EDWARD BRIDGE DANSON

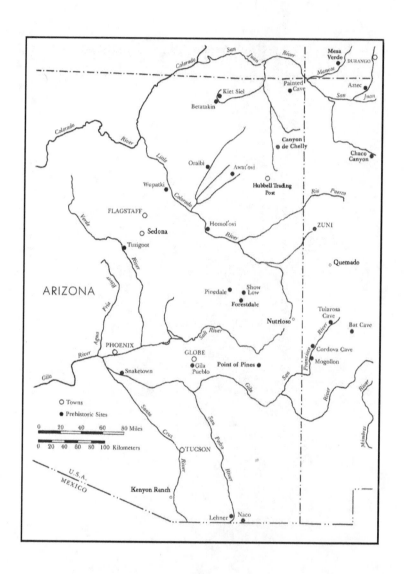

San Juan River

Colorado

Mesa Verde
● DURANGO ○

Mancos

Kiet Siel ●
Painted Cave ●
Aztec ●

Betatakin ●

San Juan

Colorado

River

Little

Canyon de Chelly ●

Chaco Canyon ●

Oraibi ●
Awat'ovi ●

Colorado

Hubbell Trading Post ○

Rio Puerco

Wupatki ●

FLAGSTAFF ○

Homol'ovi ●

ZUNI ●

River

● Sedona

Verde

Tuzigoot ●

River

Quemado ○

ARIZONA

River

Agua

Pinedale ●
Show Low ●
Forestdale ●

Tularosa Cave ●

Bat Cave ●

Nutrioso ○

Salt River

Cordova Cave ●
Mogollon ●

San

Francisco

PHOENIX ○

GLOBE ○
Gila Pueblo ●
Point of Pines ●

River

River

Snaketown ●

Gila

San Pedro

Gila

River

Mimbres

River

○ Towns
● Prehistoric Sites

0   20   40   60   80 Miles
0 20 40 60 80 100 Kilometers

Santa Cruz

River

○ TUCSON

U.S.A.
MEXICO

Kenyon Ranch ○

Lehner ●
Naco ●

EDWARD BRIDGE DANSON
Steward of the New West

Eric Penner Haury

Foreword by Ted Danson
&
Jan Danson Haury

Introduction by Robert Breunig

MUSEUM *of* NORTHERN ARIZONA
2011

Published by the Museum of Northern Arizona, Flagstaff

LIBRARY OF CONGRESS CATALOGING-IN-PUBLICATION DATA

Haury, Eric Penner, (1973-)

Title: Edward Bridge Danson: Steward of the New West / Eric Penner Haury.——1st ed.

p. cm.

Includes bibliographical references.

ISBN-13: 9780897341509
ISBN-10: 0897341503

1. Danson, Edward Bridge, Jr., 1916-2000. 2. Danson, Ned, 1916-2000. 3. Museum of Northern Arizona—History. 4. South-west—Anthropology—Biography. 5. Museology—Biography. 6. Arizona—Biography. 7. Arizona—History. 8. Danson, Ted 1947- —Family—Biography.
I. Title. II. Edward Bridge Danson: Steward of the New West.

LC Number: E76.45.C67 H79 2011
Dewey Decimal Number: 979.1

20110301

First Edition 2011

Printed in the United States of America

DEDICATED TO JAN DANSON HAURY

Daughter of this book's subject
Mother of its author
Conceiver of the project
Chief Researcher

In gratitude for her love and support

CONTENTS

FOREWORD

When the Museum of Northern Arizona (MNA) set a goal of fully funding its Edward Bridge Danson, Jr., Endowed Chair in Anthropology, named in honor of our father, its second director, we thought it was important to share our father's story with a new generation.

As children growing up in the 1950s and 60s, we knew our father best as a storyteller who loved people and enjoyed entertaining guests from all walks of life. At dinner parties, in the Museum's historic McMillan Homestead in Flagstaff, we gathered with guests around our large dining room table lit with candles. There we listened rapt as Dad regaled both the family and our visitors with stories about his childhood in Ohio or adventures as a young man traveling around the world on a schooner—celebrating Christmas on the Galapagos Islands, attending the cremation of a Balinese princess, or visiting peaceful South Pacific islands he later returned to during the height of war.

Dad traveled often on behalf of his work. Whenever he returned from professional meetings held across the nation, the family would come together in the living room during the cocktail hour to hear him tell about the people he had met, the food he had eaten and the places he had seen.

Because Dad was an archaeologist and museum director, we, unlike most children in America, were able to share parts of our father's professional life, first during three summers in the mid-1950s at Point of Pines, the University of Arizona's archaeological field school on the San Carlos Apache Indian Reservation, and later at the Museum of Northern Arizona in Flagstaff, Arizona, where Dad served as assistant director, and then director,

from 1956 to 1975. At the field school, we came to know anthropology students from universities across the country, and
two from as far away as Iraq. Jan remembers joining the students
in the evenings to listen to our father lecture on Southwestern
archaeology; and both of us recall visiting nearby sites to talk
with the students as they excavated ancestral pueblo rooms, and
looking for beads and arrowheads, which we had been taught
to hand over to the faculty. Our family shared Fourth of July
barbecues and square dances with the staff, students and Apache
cowboys from the tribe's nearby cattle ranch.

After we moved to Flagstaff in 1956, we were introduced
to artists, writers and scientists from multiple disciplines, heard
them talk about their work, and were fortunate to go on scientific field trips with some of them. Dad and Mom loved to invite
people for cocktails on the Homestead's screened porch or for
picnics on the nearby 12,000-foot-high San Francisco Peaks,
especially in the fall when the aspen leaves were turning gold.
Through our parents we became friends with cattle ranchers
from the Flagstaff area. From all of them and from our parents
we learned to appreciate the wonders of nature and the need to
preserve the earth's delicate balance.

Dad and Mom taught us to appreciate the gifts of other
cultures, not through verbal teaching, but by allowing us to experience what they have to offer the world. During summers in
Flagstaff, the main events in our family's life centered on the
Museum's Hopi and Navajo craftsmen shows. These shows were
the highlights of our year. Jan felt privileged helping the Museum staff prepare baskets, pottery and rugs for judging before
the shows began and listening as the judges talked about what
made something a prize winner. The whole family greeted visitors, directed them to the areas where different arts and crafts
were being sold and made sales.

At the Hopi shows, arts and crafts were laid out on tables
and organized by village. As we helped out or just talked to staff
and the Hopi craft demonstrators, we learned the village names

and which ones were known for which kind of basket or pottery. We saw artists carve katsina dolls, make pottery and, our favorite, bake fresh hand-ground cornmeal piki bread in the traditional way on a hot stone, which had been passed down through generations of Hopi women. Our family became friends with many of the Hopi demonstrators, who returned to the Hopi shows year after year.

During the Navajo shows, we witnessed the time and skill it took for a demonstrator to create a Navajo rug or make a piece of jewelry. Jan remembers being fascinated as she watched a medicine man let the sand flow through his fingers as he made a traditional sandpainting on the floor of the special exhibit hall.

When he could, our father took the family to Navajo trading posts and Hopi katsina dances on the mesas. Mom and Dad attended Hopi dances on Saturdays with the same reverence they brought with them to the Episcopal Church on Sundays. They taught us to respect widely different religious traditions, again, not verbally, but by letting us experience them.

Ted's best friend Raymond Coin was the son of a Hopi silversmith and Museum staff member who lived near us. On one occasion, young Ted was invited to visit the Coin family at their Hopi home on Third Mesa. Ted and Raymond drove out in the back of the Coin's truck, standing up pretending they were on a stagecoach. On the mesa, while roughhousing with his friends, Ted fell, dislocating and chipping his elbow. One of Raymond's grandfathers was a bone-setter, and he set Ted's arm. Back in Flagstaff, our parents rejoiced when Ted's doctor reported that he could not have done a better job.

While we knew about many aspects of our father's public life at the Museum, we knew little about the projects he worked on during office hours. As a teenager, Ted made a rare visit to Dad's office at the Museum's Research Center. In one or two minutes, watching him at work, Ted saw our father dealing skillfully and efficiently with his secretary and staff. He recalls thinking: *This is a powerful, effective, strong man.*

Dad was the master of any social situation, quickly turning strangers into friends, often using his sense of humor and ability to tell tales to include people in his circle. Ted recalls a family trip to Europe in 1965, when at dinner in a restaurant, Dad started out telling the family one of his stories in his loud, jovial voice. As he spoke, he noticed people at nearby tables smiling. He raised his voice to bring them into his growing audience. As a fourteen-year-old, having spent the trip devouring James Bond books, Ted recalls feeling embarrassed that his jovial father did not have Bond's smooth, suave personality. As we grew older, we realized Dad's outgoing personality was one of his gifts.

In the 1980s, Dad started writing an autobiography, beginning with his birth and ending with his first years at the Museum; this he gave to family members as a Christmas present in 1993. As we did research, we discovered Dad often used outdated terminology and spellings, which we have updated in this book, except in quotations. And the facts in his autobiography were not always reliable, for his memory was failing when he wrote it. But he was still a wonderful storyteller, and many of the stories in this book come from his unpublished autobiography.

In correcting the inaccuracies, we were fortunate that our parents had kept so many records from their past. There are dozens of family scrapbooks, which include newspaper articles as well as photos. Dad's mother and his oldest sister, Virginia Perin, saved the letters and journals he wrote on his early travels around the world and his letters home during World War II. As a well trained archaeologist, Dad also kept excellent journals of his early archaeological digs and surveys. And as director of the Museum of Northern Arizona, he wrote thorough annual reports, which provide detailed information about what was happening at the Museum and its adjacent Harold S. Colton Research Center. He also gave dozens of boxes of his correspondence from his years at the Museum to MNA's library, which helped us understand what he did, first as assistant director and later as director. And after Dad's retirement, Mother kept a brief daily journal on her calendars, which enabled us to fill in the blanks for their years living in retirement in Sedona, Arizona.

Working together on this Danson biography, written by Eric Haury, his grandson, has taught us much about the work our father did to further the goals set by the Museum's first director, Dr. Harold S. Colton, and his wife, artist Mary-Russell Ferrell Colton. Our father was a bridge between the Colton's family-run Museum and the larger independent Museum of today. He worked closely with the Coltons to maintain their dream, but as an administrator he prepared the Museum to grow so that it could meet the opportunities and needs of the future. We are excited that the Museum today, under the leadership of Dr. Robert Breunig, is continuing the dream that meant so much to its founders and which Mom and Dad worked so hard to preserve and develop.

While neither of our parents lived long enough to see Dr. Kelley Hays-Gilpin named to the Edward Bridge Danson, Jr., Endowed Chair in Anthropology, they would have been delighted with the work she is doing to bring the vision for the Museum, which meant so much to them, into the 21st century. We hope this book will further the work of the Museum and the Danson Chair as it introduces its readers to our father.

Ted Danson and Jan Danson Haury

INTRODUCTION

Edward B. "Ned" Danson was the second director of the Museum of Northern Arizona, and my predecessor. He was a museum director's director, a man of great energy, a strong spirit, and a man with a deep passion for his institution, its mission and region that it served. And, as Eric Haury so ably documents in this volume, Ned Danson not only helped build the Museum of Northern Arizona into the institution it is today, he also operated on a much wider stage throughout the region, influencing federal policies and initiatives in Arizona and the West.

I first met Ned on the Hopi Indian Reservation in 1970, while I was a graduate student in anthropology. I was living in an apartment adjacent to the home of the famous Hopi author and potter, Polingaysi Qoyawayma (Elizabeth Q. White). Ned and others from the Museum of Northern Arizona came to Elizabeth's house to stay overnight while conducting the Museum's annual collecting trip for what was then called the "Hopi Craftsman Exhibition."

I was fascinated by the entire scene. Ned, the Museum director, Jessica, his wife, and the other members of the Museum crew were going from village to village, house to house to collect items for sale at the Museum's annual exhibit. It was clear from what Ned told me about these trips, the visits to the homes, and of the event itself, that this museum—and its leadership—had a special relationship with the Hopi. Indeed, for several generations, Museum personnel went door to door, twice a year, collecting material for what we call today the "Hopi Festival of Arts and Culture." Nevertheless, Ned and Jessica Danson, and the Museum staff, following on the traditions established by

Harold and Mary-Russell Ferrell Colton, did more than collect objects; they built relationships, meaningful relationships with a wide swath of the Hopi population. Many Hopi families looked forward to these visits just as much as the Museum staff did and prepared copious quantities of art, set aside just for the Museum. Little did I imagine then that someday I would not only be myself responsible for the Hopi Show, but for the Museum itself.

Ned was also something of a tease, which stood him in good stead with many Hopi women who could give great teases back. On another collecting trip, about ten years later (when I was then, as Curator of the Museum, responsible for putting on the Hopi Show), Ned and I entered the home of the potter Rena Kavena. On spotting Rena, Ned broke into song, "Rena Kavena the belle of the ball, Rena Kavena, she danced with them all . . . !" She broke into gales of laughter. I have no idea how this song got started, but it was obvious that Ned had been singing it to Rena Kavena for many years and that she loved it.

Just a year ago, I was attending a baby-naming ceremony at Second Mesa. A man whom I did not know began talking with me. When I told him I was the director of the Museum of Northern Arizona, his face lit up. "Oh, I knew Dr. Danson, he used to come every year to my aunt's house, Rena Kavena. He would always sing this song . . . " I stopped him mid-sentence and started singing Ned's "Rena Kavena song." Then he and I had a laugh together, not unlike the laugh Ned and Rena Kavena shared so long ago.

That was Ned's special quality. He loved people, he engaged with them, and built enduring relationships with them—Hopi and Navajo, cowboys and professors, Senators and shopkeepers. He made MNA a beloved institution in the eyes of so many people who would be touched by him and pulled in by his infectious enthusiasm for the institution he led. My memories of Ned, the causes he championed, his zest for life and his work, and the meaningful relationships he nurtured still inspire me today.

This biography also connects me with Ned in other ways. He struggled with many of the same issues that confront the museum's administration today: building the endowment fund, fostering significant research programs, strengthening relationships with the region's various Indian tribes, protecting and building the collections, constantly striving to balance the operating budget, fairly compensating a highly talented but often underpaid staff, keeping members and donors informed, and most important of all, articulating a compelling vision for the future of the institution.

In honor of his many contributions to the Museum, and the discipline of archaeology, MNA has dedicated its chair in anthropology to Ned Danson. The Danson Chair of Anthropology is today occupied by Dr. Kelley Hays-Gilpin—part time, as the chair is not yet fully funded. Dr. Gilpin, also a professor of anthropology at Northern Arizona University, can only spend a portion of her time at the Museum. It is our hope that this book will inspire others to honor Ned's memory by supporting the Danson Chair campaign so that Ned's legacy of service can be appropriately honored and more fully carried forward.

Robert Breunig, Director
Museum of Northern Arizona

CHAPTER ONE

GENTLEMAN ADVENTURER
The Early Years
1916 - 1937

On March 22, 1916, a child was born to the Danson family in the community of Glendale, just outside of Cincinnati, Ohio. According to family lore, as Rufus Southworth, the family doctor, came down from the bedroom to report the birth to the child's father, he said, "It's a boy, E. B., a perfect gentleman. His hair is parted just like yours."

This was the news fifty-four-year-old Edward Bridge Danson, Sr., had wanted for years. A British immigrant and son of a Liverpool architect, his first wife had died in childbirth. His second wife, Anna Louise Allen, a member of an established Cincinnati family, had borne two daughters and now their only son.

Although they christened the boy Edward Bridge Danson, Jr., in a lasting celebration of the fulfillment of his father's dreams, the Dansons simply called him, "Boy." It would be the only name he would know for the first several years of his life. The young Danson would be told the truth only when, on a train trip, while exploring the car, he was told by the conductor, "Sit down, boy."

Amazed, he went to his parents and asked them, "How did he know my name?"

And so "Boy" became "Ned."

But even before he learned his name, the future anthropologist had already begun to observe his first culture, that of

Danson family. (Left to right) Virginia, Edward Bridge Sr., Ann, Ann Allen and Edward Bridge Jr. ("Boy")

the Glendale society surrounding him. It was a culture little changed from the Victorian Era, one of traditions and taboos, one in which people wore different clothing in morning, after-noon, and evening; girls when they came to a certain age, were formally presented to polite society at ritualized social gather-ings; men such as the senior Danson regularly traveled to the country to hunt quail for sport; and houses were built with two dining rooms, one for the family, one for staff. The Danson's household included a cook, a maid, a laundress, a nanny when the children were young, and Arthur Coleman, who was a butler, chauffeur and gardener.

Danson absorbed this culture surrounded by family—not merely his parents and sisters, but numerous Allen aunts, uncles, cousins and his maternal grandfather, William Mercer Allen, a banker and philanthropist who supported Cincinnati's Chil-dren's Hospital and Glendale's Bethany Home for Boys. The

"Boy" on running board of family Buick, 1918

Ned at Tryon, North Carolina

relatives all had a role in introducing him to this society. Some would later play a role in helping him leave it.

Danson's immediate family lived in two different houses over the course of his youth. The house where he was born was across the street from his grandparents' home. The second, designed by his father, had six bedrooms and was on land large enough for Mrs. Danson to plant 3,000 bulbs around the edge of the grounds. The family regularly made good use of their property for entertaining. Danson recalled that both of his parents loved to socialize and invited large groups of friends over to their house for regular dinner parties. Some of his earliest memories were of sitting in his pajamas at the top of the stairs, watching guests in their evening clothes arrive at one of his parents' parties. As he grew older, he began to be invited down for gradually increasing amounts of time, an early introduction to the love of socializing that would permeate his life. Danson recalled, in this age of Prohibition, being given sips from his father's martini glass. The gin for the martinis was produced quietly in a bathtub by the family and a group of friends.

But while this law was flouted in the Danson household, other, often unwritten, rules were obeyed. E. B. Danson felt a moral obligation to help those less fortunate. On numerous occasions, Ned Danson recalled seeing his father give financial assistance to British immigrants and expatriates in need, whether due to bad fortune or their own poor choices. And to prevent his son from making similarly poor choices, the elder Danson taught his son never to make a loan you cannot afford to lose.

"They were not people of great wealth," Ned Danson later wrote of his family, "but they certainly were comfortable and we lived well, were educated well . . . and were used to 'the good life.'" From receiving gold diaper pins and an ivory teething ring as an infant, to travels to summer resorts, to living in a home with two cars in an era before most people even had one, Danson readily absorbed the values and manners of that culture. And in his youth, he showed all the signs of becoming a gentleman, though not necessarily the perfect one that his first hairstyle predicted.

When he was about five, he bit his last nanny on the fanny, and after that the biting continued. One day, at about the same age, while out in the garden, he invited one of his elder sisters to put her finger in his mouth. She refused, naturally assuming that he would bite it. He promised not to, and she did as he requested.

Her cry of pain alerted their father. Young Danson was ordered to put his own finger in his father's mouth and receive the punishment of a finger for a finger. The lesson Ned reported learning was: "never to bite a finger when someone who can bite you harder is nearby."

But Danson did not merely want to skirt the confining rules of the world to which he was born—he wanted adventure. To him, even going to his room could become an adventure. He often ran up the stairs and leapt through the door of his bedroom to flop on his bed, a dangerous maneuver, especially on the day that his family had rearranged the room without telling him. He had a scar on his head for the rest of his life.

The bedroom into which he had leapt contained a library filled with books that fed his love of adventure, such as *Treasure Island, Beyond Khyber Pass, David Goes to Greenland* and *Lindbergh Flies On!* Other books like *From Columbus to Lincoln: A Selection of Letters and other Historical Accounts by People of Note who Lived at the Time of the Events* focused on encouraging readers to put themselves in a historical context and to learn character from those of the past.

His family did not shrink from adventures, at least tame ones. They escaped both the cold of Cincinnati's winters and the heat of its summers. In the summers, Ned went to camps on the Great Lakes with his mother and sisters, joined by his father on the weekends. He recalled attending family camps, such as Castle Park in Michigan, which had an imitation Greek amphitheater and invited its guests to participate in putting on plays; and also Grand Island Forest, an early game preserve overlooking Lake

6 EDWARD BRIDGE DANSON

Superior. When he grew older, Ned attended summer camps for boys in Michigan and Maine. The Dansons traveled twice to visit their father's family in Britain and also stayed in many country homes in the United States belonging to his Ohio family or his parents' numerous friends.

The winter months after Christmas were invariably spent in Tryon, North Carolina, where the climate was much better for Mrs. Danson's asthma. In North Carolina, young Ned joined his mother and sisters in riding horses through the mountain country and enjoyed early wilderness excursions in a life that would later take him to rural areas for archaeological digs.

It was in Tryon that Danson also recalled first noticing the Jim Crow rules, watching African-Americans cross the street to make way for him and his mother whenever they walked down the roads. He recalled asking his parents why society was arranged that way. He decided that he did not approve. This was an early sign of his belief in fair treatment for all people. Even though he would always exhibit the manners and social graces of the world in which he was born, he would embrace the democratizing changes that were to come in American society.

The young boy's horizons expanded further in the summer of 1926, when his family traveled to the American Southwest and took one of the first Fred Harvey "Southwest Indian Detours." They followed this with a visit to relatives in Santa Monica, California, and with another guided tour through Northern California. Although, later in life, his memories of the experience were faint, it was the first encounter this young boy would have with the people and places of Arizona, which he would know and love for so long. He did recall visiting the Grand Canyon, experiencing a rodeo, attending Indian dances, visiting archaeological sites, and spending the night in Hubbell Trading Post, a working trading post whose destiny he would later change. He also recalled loving the touring cars in which they drove.

Ned (second from left) at Grand Canyon, Arizona, 1926

Ned (far right) on touring car in Sequoia National Park, 1926

The Southwest had a very different environment and culture from the Southern-influenced, Midwestern city he knew so well. And it made an impression on him. Although he did not remember it, a family friend, also on the trip, said that he told her that he wanted to become an anthropologist when he grew up. Whether this was momentary impulse or the first sign of a lasting drive, inspired by the people and places he had visited, the words would prove true.

Young Ned's father was head of the Kemper-Thomas Calendar and Novelty Company, an advertising manufacturer, one of the first companies to produce promotional items bearing the names of client companies. Family lore claimed that the company introduced the yo-yo and the mechanical pencil to the United States and was one of the first to use billboards along roads. His company also produced advertising calendars that featured reproductions of paintings. For many years, the senior Danson sought permission from New York's Metropolitan Museum of Art to use some of their paintings in his calendars. "Every year," his son later recalled:

> he would go to the Metropolitan Museum and take with him samples of the latest methods of color reproduction. He would sit with the Metropolitan curators of art and experts to review the process. For many years they would say it is not good enough, but finally twenty years after he started, they finally allowed him to reproduce a painting from the Metropolitan Museum Collection.

This was one of the first calendars to duplicate fine art from a major museum. Those trips to New York were just some of the many causes that regularly took Ned's father away from home during the boy's youth.

However, in 1923, the senior Danson started taking his son with him to work. Years later, Ned Danson fondly recalled these visits:

He used to take me to the office almost every Saturday when he was home. . . . I loved to drive with him and he would talk to me. . . . Those Saturdays have sort of stuck in my mind for they meant going to the factory, where I always enjoyed looking at everything, especially the sample room, and then we'd go into the city, have lunch at the Queen City Club, have our hair trimmed, buy fish . . . and sweet rolls for Sunday's breakfast.

Along with those rolls, young Danson came back with an experience of how his father ran a successful company. "I don't think I knew what he was doing," Danson concluded, "but I realize now that he was trying to prepare me for life. . . ."

And E. B. Danson had cause to give his son extra attention. He did not have much time to do so. "Back in the summer of 1923," Ned Danson wrote, "Daddy must have had some sort of a stroke. . . . I think [he] knew he was not going to live long." In February, 1927, E. B. Danson, Sr., died from a stroke and kidney failure. Young Ned was not quite eleven.

After his father's death, Ned was the senior male Danson, but it was Arthur Coleman, the chauffeur, who became the effective man of the house, as well as young Danson's next model for how to be a good man. Even before his father's death, Ned had been close to Coleman.

Coleman was many things to the family. Danson recalled as a child watching him carefully polishing the family silver, a task Ned loved to do himself later in life. Coleman watched the young boy when need be, leading him away from places where people might be discussing indelicate topics. But perhaps his most important role, from Ned's perspective, was as keeper of the family's cars.

Cars were Ned Danson's first love. They combined his desire for adventure with his love of beauty. He enjoyed looking at them, reading about them, playing with toy cars and riding in real ones. One of his first toys in the cradle had been a car. In

Ned in "first pair of long pants," 1928

his youth, he cut pictures of cars out of magazines and arranged them in a scrapbook he would keep for the rest of his life. Since he had been raised before the advent of driver's licenses, he started driving young, serving as his mother's driver for their annual winter trek to North Carolina when he was fourteen.

In addition to all the other things cars were to him, in his teenage years, they were a sort of fashion accessory, just like the tailored suits, ties and evening clothes he loved to wear. He had already cultivated the sense of style that would later lead people to call him dapper and dashing. But he combined this sense with an indifference to formal schooling. "I liked to play and . . . I hated to study," Danson recalled. "I did like to read and I read continuously, but I wasn't, nor ever was, an intellectual reader."

As his mother put it during one of their arguments, "You've been playing hooky. You've not been serious, you've just been playing. You haven't been studying and I know it."

Although most of the schools he attended—or did not attend, as the case may be—were in Cincinnati, he spent a year at the Asheville School in North Carolina, disinterested in his studies but cultivating his aesthetic senses. For twenty-five dollars, he bought three Chinese horse print scrolls (one from the 1700s and two from the early 1800s) from a teacher who had a brother serving as a missionary in China—another early sign of his interest, both in beauty and in cultures far beyond his own.

At the end of the year, despite his poor grades, Danson was offered a scholarship by the Asheville School. It would have been helpful, for although far better off than most, his family was not immune to the Great Depression. Their staff had been reduced from five to two—Arthur Coleman and Gertrude Carter, their cook and maid.

Yet young Ned Danson did an unusual thing. "I said that [the Asheville School was] doing that only because of the people we knew, not because I was a good student," he later wrote. "So it was decided that I would go back to Cincinnati." He did not want to accept something he felt he had not earned.

Danson took his first major trip without his family in 1932 at age sixteen, joining members from the Episcopal Brotherhood of St. Andrew for two weeks in Japan. He attended lectures at the University of Tokyo and traveled across the country. As was already his habit, he started looking for objects of aesthetic and historical interest. As he later wrote:

> We went to a shop owned by a Japanese *obi* [sash] dealer. His *obis* were used by the Imperial family. I bought two of them, one, a lovely old [*obi*] that had a background of tarnished silver threads in beige silk. . . . I bought a black pearl and a white pearl for $5.00, and they are now in my mother's diamond and pearl ring. . . . In a junk shop in Osake [sic], I found a gold embroidered white and beige square cloth with tassels at the corners. I bought it for twenty-five cents. . . . I found out that the gold

embroidery is the Shogunate Seal, and that it was a "gift cloth" used in the old days to carry a gift.

Back in the United States, Danson continued his life of high style and lackluster academics until a foolish stunt with his car radically altered his life. Just before Halloween in 1933, he and one of his Allen cousins raced to school in their cars, as they often did. Years later, he recalled what happened:

> I didn't know that the front tires of [my car] were smooth, and in taking the curve on Clifton Hill the front end didn't go round the bend. It simply shot across the road. [My cousin], who was behind me, passed me on the right laughing. Three cars that were coming down the hill towards me went off into somebody's lawn. I put the car into first and tore after [my cousin].

By the time Ned left school that afternoon, he had forgotten the incident. Upon his return home, he found his mother, stern-faced, waiting for him at the door. Danson recalled, " . . . my mother was a very handsome woman, but sometimes she could look like a black cloud—and she was like a black kind of cloud that night."

She held out her hand, saying, "I want the keys, please," and then informed her son that he would not be allowed to drive for the next month.

When he protested that he had a date for a big dance that weekend, she replied, "I believe you skidded this morning."

"How did you know?" Danson asked.

"I was in the third car," she told him.

After a long argument in which he recalled that his mother "wasn't giving an inch," the telephone rang. His mother went to answer it. The man on the other end was Rufus Southworth, the doctor who had delivered Danson. He was calling to make an offer to the young man he had helped bring into the world.

When the conversation ended, Mrs. Danson returned to her son with a choice. Either he could be grounded for a month, or he could join Dr. Southworth as part of the crew on the schooner *Yankee*, which was about to leave for an eighteen-month voyage circumnavigating the world.

"Maybe it's time you got away," he recalled her saying. "I don't know that I can handle you alone."

Ned Danson and his mother arrived in the port of Gloucester, Massachusetts, a few days before the ship was to sail. At seventeen, he was the youngest of the crew. In his fifties, Dr. Southworth was the oldest. The *Yankee* was captained by Irving Johnson, with his wife, Electa "Exy" Johnson, serving as first mate. Irving Johnson had previously sailed around Cape Horn, but this was the first of what would eventually be seven trips the couple would take around the world. This experience would be new for everyone on board.

Upon arriving on the ship, Danson put his "good summer white suit in the closet" and wrote to his sister, Ann:

> Yesterday afternoon I came on board and unpacked with Mother's help. My berth is . . . in the middle and it's very comfortable. The ship is really fascinating and I really think I can be very happy here for 18 months. I seem to be in a dream. I can't realize that Ned Danson is going around the world for 18 months on a schooner.

Despite his disbelief, the ninety-foot vessel left port with a crew of fifteen on November 5, 1933, at 2:05 P.M. The voyage took Danson across four oceans and to four continents with stops at numerous islands along the way. A few members of the crew left before the end and others joined, but the number of crew stayed near fifteen for the entire trip, four of them women.

"We were passengers, crew, and guests all in one," Exy Johnson wrote in her book, *Westward Bound in the Schooner* Yankee.

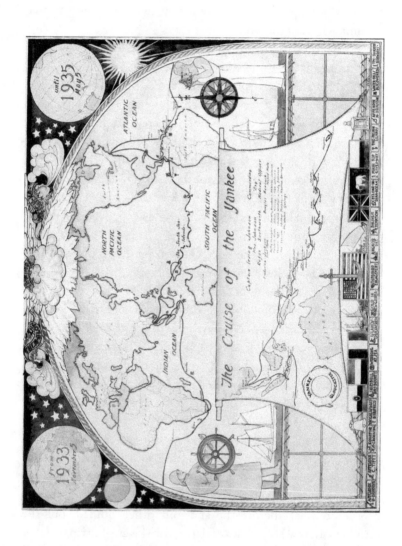

Schooner Yankee

Captain Irving Johnson and wife Exy on the Yankee

Yankee crew. (Ned sitting, top row second from left, Dr. Southworth top row center)

Yankee crew at work (Ned far left)

"Whatever the *Yankee* did would be due to nothing but our own efforts. The main decisions always rested with the Skipper. The [two] mates were in regular sea-going command over their watches, and everyone had a real part in the responsibility of sailing the ship." Each member of the crew paid a share of the expenses.

Throughout the adventure, Ned used every opportunity available to him to send pages from his diary back to his mother and sisters to report on what he was experiencing. After passing through the Panama Canal, they sailed south. On Christmas day, Danson recorded in his journal, "One of the best presents the ship got was given by our watch (the 4 to 8) this morning. It was the first sight of Galapagos. . . . The island, San Cristobal, which is to be our first stop, is slowly gliding by us." He gave it one of his highest compliments: "It is perfectly beautiful."

While exploring the Galapagos, islands that had inspired Darwin, they saw iguanas, collected sea turtles for food and, as Danson wrote his family, "took loads of movies of the seals and sea lions in the water and on the shore. We caught a baby sea lion about three feet long and took him out to the boat. He was very happy and hated to go back at night."

Little more than three weeks later, the *Yankee* had crossed 3,000 miles of the Pacific and arrived at the island of Pitcairn, where the descendants of the *H.M.S. Bounty* mutineers still lived. Danson recorded his visit in his journal:

> There is no place to anchor so all of us couldn't go ashore at one time. I went in the morning. It was very exciting going in as the wind was blowing and the boat was pitching and rolling. . . . The bay where they land is very very thrilling to land in. There are rocks on all sides and enormous breakers were tumbling all over them. We waited until a lull came in between the breakers and then in we went. The breakers caught up with us and we just planed in to the beach missing rocks on all sides by a narrow margin.

Bounty Bay, Pitcairn Island, 1934

Pitcairn Islanders ferrying Yankee *crew*

After the harrowing arrival, they met the island's leader, Parkin Christian. The Pitcairn people held a feast for their visitors and invited them to stay in their homes. Danson wrote that they "were the most hospitable people I've ever met. . . ."

Perhaps they were almost too hospitable. Having settled into the home of a Mr. Waring, Danson was invited by his host to take a walk up the mountain to where the islanders kept the gardens. He described the walk in a letter to his family.

> Mr. Waring would give me a pineapple to eat and after finishing that he would hand me 5 or 6 peaches. All together on that walk I ate 8 peaches, 2 pineapples, 6 rose apples . . . I passion fruit, 2 mangoes and half a watermelon. When we got back to the house about 2 o'clock we sat down to dinner and I ate a piece of pumpkin pie, a piece of peach pie a whole chicken, fried potatoes, corn, tomatoes and tea and hot peach juice besides bread and butter. Then they wanted to know why I didn't eat more.

The *Yankee* crew stayed two days with the Pitcairners, trading with them and seeing the recently rediscovered rudder of the *Bounty* that had sunk in 1779. Then the ship left this community, founded by British exiles and their Tahitian companions, and sailed east for Mangareva, both culturally and geographically the first South Sea Island they would visit.

They spent the next six months sailing from island to island in the South Pacific—some of the islands uncharted before their visits—stopping at such places as Tahiti and Tonga, sailing by the New Hebrides and near an island named Bougainville, which Danson would visit in different circumstances less than a decade later.

Throughout his journey, Danson encountered many living cultures far different from his own. Some of the communities had met no people of European ancestry before the *Yankee's*

Vao drummer, Vanuatu Island, New Hebrides, 1934

Wall frieze, Angkor Thom, Cambodia

arrival. As he encountered cultures with a variety of traditions, he recorded the details of what he witnessed in both his journal and his letters home. His curiosity about other peoples and talent for spotting details would later serve him well as an anthropologist.

In Vao, one of the New Hebrides islands, he described a dance held under a full moon beneath giant banyan trees:

> We walked along a path thro[sic] the jungle and the farther we went the louder became the drums. . . . Suddenly we rounded a rocky knoll and there we came to the dance place. . . . The drums would start slowly and softly and the dancers would start a low chant . . . swaying back and forth. . . . As the drums grew faster the dancers rocked faster and the chanting grew louder. . . . Finally with a great roar the dancers rushed around . . . yelling their heads off. Suddenly they would stop, the drums quiet. . . . Then . . . repeating the dance over and over.

A few days later at Utupua, in the Solomon Islands, as Danson explored a village, he not only noted what appealed to his aesthetics, observing that "the houses were oval shaped and nicely woven. . . ," but also showed interest in cultural details. "The young unmarried men," he wrote, "have a house all to themselves. . . . It is made of red, black and white woven palm fronds." He concluded that it was "Easily the nicest house in the village."

As the *Yankee* continued through the Solomon Islands, Danson suffered a case of appendicitis. The young man who had been given even more than he could eat while on Pitcairn reported in a letter to his family that, "I'm on a starvation diet, water and nothing else but water. . . . There'll be no need of an operation Brick [Dr. Southworth] says, so long as it doesn't get worse." Ned recovered and was soon back at his duties.

When their time in the South Pacific was finished, Danson reflected on the beauty and adventure he had experienced and wrote in his journal with characteristic exuberance, "Today we said goodbye to the South Sea Islands. . . . We've seen many interesting and beautiful things. I'll never forget these months. They've been nearly perfect. . . . Goodbye South Seas. Thank God for your beauty. Even civilization cannot take that away from you. It's yours for always. It's incomparable. Keep it."

Their time along the coast of Indo-China included a stop in Bangkok and a visit to the Angkor Complex in Cambodia. "We went by Angkor Wat . . . to the Bayon, one of the best pre-served temples besides Angkor. . . . The walls of the outer gallery are all beautifully carved and . . . represent the everyday life of the Khmers. . . . You could spend hours looking at the different pictures. We climbed all over it and the building is really remarkable." He compared its quality to that of masterworks from Western culture, saying, "Stretching north of the Bayon for meters is what compares with the Circus Maximus in Rome," and declared, "there is so much we didn't see that I'm positive I'm coming back here and stay a month some day." He summed up with: "Angkor, gosh but it is wonderful."

In Bali, he had the good fortune to attend a rarely held cer-emony. It was a mass cremation in which the body of a Balinese princess was the most prominent person to be burned. "Some bodies," he wrote, "are preserved twenty or more years as no one can be burned before the oldest member of the family." The *Yankee* crew watched with fascination as the procession of towers carrying the bodies twisted and turned through the streets in an attempt to "fool the devils."

Danson saw Balinese cock fights and dances, noting with ob-vious admiration, as someone who loved to dance, that "There are little girls who do . . . a beautiful and rhythmic dance that would try an old and experienced dancer to do in any other country."

But Danson was not simply a tourist on this voyage. He worked. "Everyone about except Fritz [the cook] stood watch," he recalled, "four hours on and eight off from the beginning of the trip till the end." Along the way, Danson observed Irving

Balinese dancer

Balinese cremation tower

Balinese cremation bulls

Johnson's leadership style and absorbed lessons on how to run an institution, whether it be a ship or—in his case, years later—a museum. "In watches as in everything else the cruise was run on two main principles: to have a good time," Exy Johnson wrote, "and to sail the ship properly. . . . If somebody didn't do anything on watch once in a while, it was no crime."

Danson must have slacked off more than once in a while, for seven months into the voyage, Johnson wrote to Danson's mother.

> I have had a good many personal talks with Ned during the cruise and amongst other things have bawled him out a number of times, all of which he has taken in the right spirit and he has never caused us any trouble in port or aboard ship. When we arrive in Gloucester next May, if you will come to me, I will point out Ned. He has changed so much I doubt you will know him. . . . He is just plain growing up in the healthiest kind of way and Exy and I think he shows great promise as a young man. Ned has shown a good deal of independence in his thought and convictions and, though his physical alertness is below average, this is speeding up appreciably and he has always had extreme mental alertness.

As well as studying other cultures, Ned Danson, ever the devotee of the social graces, made sure to follow his own society's mores. Writing to his mother from Fiji, he said, "I now find that I will need a dress jacket in Bangkok and Singapore. As we have letters of introduction to people high up in the government we will need evening clothes, in fact we could use them now. That is why I've asked you to send evening pants, sox, stiff shirt wing collar, studs and a white tie. In that way all I'll need to buy is the jacket itself."

The *Yankee* berthed in Singapore and remained there around three weeks for minor maintenance. And during that time, Danson wore his new jacket on more occasions than for meetings with officials. He and others in the crew partied every night, even near the end of their stay. In a letter to his family, he described a typical Singapore evening for the crew:

> Got all rigged up in my new evening clothes, which, if I do say so, did look nice. Dottie [part of the *Yankee's* crew] and I had a table right opposite the entrance to the dance floor. The dance floor is open on two sides and is just like a big porch. Very cool and gay and in the evening when people are there in evening clothes, dancing to a good band, it is really fine. About eleven [two other crew members] came in and joined our table. After the dance was over we all went out to the swimming club and danced there until about three-thirty.

While on the ship, Danson used his time, when not on watch, reading books such as *War and Peace*, *The Forsyte Saga* and a number of histories; playing cards; and conversing with Dr. Southworth—whom Irving Johnson described as becoming a surrogate father to the young man.

After leaving the East Indies, the *Yankee* crossed the Indian Ocean, with stops in several islands and South Africa. They rounded the Cape of Good Hope, then sailed across the South Atlantic, hugging the South American coast for much of the trip north. While off British Guiana, Danson suffered a second attack of appendicitis. This time surgery was necessary, and he had to leave the boat for a tropical hospital in Georgetown. Exy Johnson described his departure in her book:

> Three or four days of starvation had not weakened the fastidious spirit that had long ago earned him the name of the "Duke" and he left the boat in style amidst general admiration for his air of elegance from the exquisite tilt of his swanky hat to the tip of his Malacca cane. Besides we were all aware of his imposing supply of Chi-

nese silk pajamas with gorgeous dragons and we realized
what a treat was in store for the hospital.

When ready to resume his travels, Danson rejoined the crew
and remained with the ship as it sailed north through the West
Indies back to the United States.

After an eighteen-month cruise, the *Yankee* returned to
Gloucester on May 5, 1935, at 2:10 PM, a mere ten minutes
later than had been scheduled at the trip's beginning. Danson
left the ship with friendships that would last a lifetime and an
experience few could match. What he did not return with was a
high school diploma.

Sailing on the *Yankee* had prevented him from completing
his senior year of high school, and this created a problem when
he applied, at his mother's insistence, to attend Cornell. When
she asked what he wanted to do after his trip, Danson said that
he " . . . thought it would be nice to travel and write. She agreed
that it would be nice, but thought that I had better go to college to at least learn how to spell, as I had been misspelling the
word 'sweet' the entire time I was gone, calling her 'My dear
sweat Mother.'"

Cornell agreed to admit him without a high school diploma,
as long as he tutored in English, Math and History. "So that
summer," he wrote, "I went in every day to Cincinnati in the
morning, tutored for three hours, came back, prepared my as-
signments, and then the next day went and tutored in two other
courses. . . . I did that six days a week for two months, and I
think I learned to study that summer."

However, as he was checking into his Cornell dorm room,
he received a call from the Dean's office telling him that he must
pass exams in both English and Math. Although Danson explained the deal that had been reached, the Dean's office was
quite insistent, and so he took both exams the next day. He
passed the English exam.

For Math, he received a "26."

Ned Danson in his 1929 Kissel roadster with Delta Upsilon fraternity brothers at Cornell University

Danson was offered the chance to take the Math exam again, and scored a "25," which he thought "showed a measure of consistency." But Cornell was not moved.

While he was packing his bags, Danson learned about a nearby tutoring school and spent the entirety of the semester studying for the Math exam. When he took it, he scored a "98." He confessed that, despite all his effort, he still did not truly know algebra. He had simply memorized the answer to each problem.

He officially entered Cornell in the spring semester of 1936 as a history major. Ever the master of social situations, Danson had already convinced the Delta Upsilon fraternity to let him pledge before entering the university. Now that he was admitted, he moved into the fraternity house and started his formal studies.

Despite the effort he had spent in getting into college, Danson found Cornell disappointing. He later claimed to remember little of his time there. His clearest recollection was of buying a "1929 Kissel Kar Kountry Klub roadster," which decades later he could describe down to the color of the wheels.

At the end of his second year at Cornell, Danson was given another offer. This came from his uncle, Bill Allen. Like Danson's mother, Bill Allen suffered from asthma. And so to escape the climate of Cincinnati, he had moved far to the west.

To Arizona.

Together, his uncle and mother had purchased some desert land south of Tucson, which Allen intended to turn into a dude ranch. He named the place Kenyon Ranch after his alma mater, Kenyon College, and needed some young men to come out and help construct additional buildings. Danson and two of his Allen cousins were enlisted to help.

They drove out to Arizona in July, 1937. Their car, which Danson remembered was a Ford sedan, boiled over every fifty miles during the Texas leg of their trip, which led them to try driving at night. Thus, Danson " . . . was awake at 5:00 in the morning as we came out of the canyon west of Bisbee and up on the plateau to Tombstone." He recalled that, "There was a pink and blue pre-sunrise sky with some fleecy white clouds, a hill with a coyote on it—I know it's melodramatic, but that's the way it was."

"It was there that I fell in love with Arizona," Danson wrote. "Somehow I knew that Arizona was going to be my home."

Bill and Sis Allen at Kenyon Ranch

Ned taking a break from building the ranch, 1937

Ned riding Buck at Kenyon Ranch

CHAPTER TWO

LOVE AND WAR
Arizona and Archaeology, With Interuption
1937 - 1956

Ned Danson's first days as an Arizonan were filled with work, heavy manual labor. New to the Southwest's summer heat, he joined his cousins, and the local men his uncle hired, in remodeling Kenyon Ranch's original house and adding several adobe and stone casitas so his uncle could attract customers from well-to-do families.

The ranch covered almost 1,000 acres of the Santa Cruz Valley in Southern Arizona, near Tubac, a small town settled by the Spanish as a garrison in 1752. A high desert land of rolling hills and mesquite trees with numerous arroyos (small ravines dug by rarely flowing streams), it was bordered on the west by the Tumacacori Mountains and on the east by the Santa Rita Mountains, with peaks over 8,000 feet high. The ranch was adjacent to a seemingly endless stretch of the Coronado National Forest.

As well as helping with the construction, Ned became his uncle's driver, taking him on trips to Tucson or Nogales or simply visiting other ranches in the Santa Cruz Valley. Many of the local landowners were wealthy Easterners. A nearby neighbor had been a General Motors executive. Two ladies, sharing a house, were, respectively, heiresses to a brandy company and to a dry goods company. And Bill Allen made sure to maintain good relations with all of them.

Ned Danson, being Ned Danson, socialized as well. He did try to stay away from what he called the "booze crowd," but he admitted to attending one of their Friday night cocktail parties. He left at 2:30 A.M. Saturday, though the party did not formally end until Monday afternoon.

Bill Allen and his nephew made connections with the local Latino community. They frequently visited the home of an elderly matriarch of the community. "It was very important then," Danson recalled, "to have good relations with the Spanish-speaking Valley people. They supplied the cooks and maids, the gardeners and general workmen for the valley, and if they didn't like you, you were 'help-less.'" But as well as understanding the need for maintaining relations with an important community, Ned was captivated by the stories she told. "Uncle Bill and I spent many hours talking with her," he recalled, "and learning some of the local history." From her stories, Danson gained an understanding of the interactions of Native peoples with the Spanish and later the Anglos, along with details about the origins and histories of local landmarks. Ned and his uncle also struck up a friendly relationship with the foreman helping to build the ranch, a man named Pepe Figueras.

On free afternoons, Danson explored the land. He searched on horseback for potential routes for guests to go on trail rides. For fun, he drove his car across the countryside on roads that shifted rapidly between safe and perilous. He spent days searching for lost mines that rumor held were there to be found, just as he would later search the land for archaeological sites. At the end of the summer, Danson went with a friend on a car trip around Arizona and New Mexico, sleeping each night under the stars.

But amidst all these adventures, Danson did not abandon formal education. In the spring of 1938, he transferred his college credits from Cornell to the University of Arizona in Tucson. Although he enrolled as a history major, when choosing his courses he picked whatever he thought might interest him. One of these courses was Introductory Anthropology.

Soon after starting Anthropology I-A, Danson encountered his teacher, Dr. Emil W. Haury, in the hall. "I . . . told him that I was really enjoying the course. . . . About a month later, he met me in the hall and asked me if I were still enjoying Anthropology I-A. I told him, more than any course I'd ever taken."

That short conversation was the beginning of one of the key relationships in Danson's life. Dr. Haury or "Doc," as Danson would call him until receiving his own Ph.D., would be first teacher and mentor, then friend, and eventually, with the marriage of two of their children, family.

Shortly after that conversation, Haury approached his student once more and asked him if he would be interested in joining an expedition to Painted Cave, a cliff dwelling in the Lukachukai Mountains in northeastern Arizona. Danson agreed.

It was a two-day drive with a caravan of three cars. Ned Danson drove his Chevrolet coach accompanied by another student, Arnold "Arnie" Withers. Emil Haury drove the University's Ford truck, and William Fulton, founder of the Amerind Foundation, was behind the wheel of the third. After spending the night in a Harvey House hotel near Gallup, they went off on such a narrow road that Danson remembered seeing the wheels of one of the cars rise up off the track as it rounded a sharp turn. After a second night, the group continued on an even worse road up to Painted Cave.

Danson wrote that, "The walls of the cave were covered with painted figures of men, hands, lightning, snakes etc. . . . Some were blackish brown, many were in fine red, and some in white or turquoise." Each member of the expedition was given a spot to dig and soon the fine, red sandstone dust was flying. They recovered many artifacts, including numerous examples of pots and a turkey feather blanket.

After spending two days at the site, the group returned to Tucson. Ned Danson resumed his studies, living at Kenyon Ranch and commuting forty miles to the University several days a week to take classes. But he was no longer a history major. For

Emil W. Haury, 1937

Painted Cave Expedition, 1938. (Left to right) Emil Haury, worker, Carr Tuthill, Ned Danson, Navajo guide, Arnie Withers, William Fulton

the second time in so brief a period he had fallen in love, this time with anthropology and archaeology.

Ned did engage in more conventional forms of romance during his time at Kenyon Ranch. In 1939, one of the many guests was a young woman from a wealthy Long Island family named "Tinker" Bell. And while he socialized with all of the visitors, he found himself spending more and more time with Tinker. "Every weekend at the ranch, we would go down to Nogales, or to a dance at . . . a cowboy nightclub," he recalled. "Dancing, a few drinks, some mild necking, and we were 'in love.'"

During the summer, with some time off, Danson visited her family in their Long Island home. He recalled being amazed to discover that their estate had an escalator from the house down to the yacht dock on their private beach.

The romance with Tinker did not last. But Ned Danson's romance with both Arizona and anthropology did.

In the late 1930s, the U of A's Department of Anthropology was small. Many of the students became close friends. Danson stayed in touch with a good number of them for decades afterward—Arnold Withers, Rex Gerald and Tom Cain, later curator of anthropology at Phoenix's Heard Museum.

In addition to the classwork Haury assigned to his students, he often took them on weekend field trips. He also ran a summer field school for his students at Forestdale on the Fort Apache Indian Reservation, which Danson attended in 1939 and 1940. At Forestdale, anthropology students were taught not only through lectures but also by the hands-on experience of carefully excavating, properly recording and preserving archaeological evidence. Haury supplemented the field work with lectures given every Sunday, a tradition that came to be known as "Sunday School."

"He certainly makes learning a pleasure . . . ," Ned wrote to his mother, "he asked us the other day if we wanted the lectures. Everyone voted for more of them." But Danson learned more from Emil Haury and Forestdale than just how to be an archaeologist. Each summer, the Forestdale camp became a small

University of Arizona's Forestdale Field School, 1939. (Danson second from right, back row)

Excavated kiva at Forestdale

community, composed of students, several teachers and a small staff. The young student watched as Haury made sure that the field school was run well. And he absorbed these lessons, along with the others. Haury was so impressed with his student that he wrote to Mrs. Danson, saying:

> Field work, as you know, is the time a person's capabilities may be appraised better than at any other time, and after working with Ned this summer, I am firmly convinced by temperament and ability he is capable of carrying on in this field. In addition to this, he possesses a personality which allows him to work admirably with others. Everyone in camp enjoyed him and on more than one occasion he proved to be the "life of the party."

After a week of digging, mapping and analyzing what they had found at Forestdale, Haury sometimes took the students on weekend field trips to other archaeological sites. In 1939, he took them on a trip north to the site of Awat'ovi, an abandoned Hopi village. On the trip up, Danson continued to admire the beauty of his adopted state, writing, "The road itself was terrible but the scenery was marvelous—one place in particular. We came over the brow of a hill down into a valley in the center of which rose a tall, steep mountain. It was a dull black and where the rains had eroded the lava away, a bright orange-red showed through. . . ."

They arrived at Awat'ovi in the evening and, after a hurried meeting with the team of archaeologists, slept that night by the site. The next morning, they were given a tour of the excavations by a man who would become another of Ned Danson's key mentors, John Otis "Jo" Brew of Harvard's Peabody Museum. The young archaeologist recorded the day in his journal:

> Mr. Brew took us on a tour of the ruin. It's a big one, 23 acres in extent and was used from Pueblo II times [ca 1000 CE] up through the arrival of the Spanish. There

are three ruins of Spanish churches and a friary besides the pueblo. The Hopi lived there until 1700 and then they all left and moved on over to the next mesa—where they live today. The expedition has been digging for five years and this is their last one.

Danson marveled at the site's features and was pleased to learn that every Saturday night, members of the Awat'ovi expedition went to a nearby trading post to relax, dance and play the piano.

After his summer in the field, Ned Danson returned to classwork. He received his Bachelor of Arts degree in May of 1940 and began taking graduate classes in anthropology at the University of Arizona in the fall. Anthropology changed him, giving him a purpose and the academic discipline he had shown before only in brief bursts.

Throughout the next few years, Danson meshed his skills and interests, often serving as Haury's driver whenever his professor needed to go into the field or conduct business elsewhere in Arizona or New Mexico. During his second summer at Forestdale, Dr. Haury asked his student to drive him to Flagstaff. A small town dominated by ranching and logging, Flagstaff grew up along the train tracks in a part of Northern Arizona 7,000 feet above sea level. While there, Ned Danson visited the Museum of Northern Arizona for the first time. The Museum, located in the shadows of the San Francisco Peaks, mountains sacred to many Native peoples of the region, was founded officially in 1928 and dedicated to the study of the land and peoples of the area that surrounded it.

In a letter to his mother, Danson declared that the museum he would one day run was "one of the nicest I've ever seen. They had a fine exhibit of water colors and another of some new Hopi silver work, where I bought [my sister] Ann's birthday or Christmas present. . . . 'Doc' and I had supper at [the home of the director and his wife] and then drove on back to camp. It was a grand drive and I certainly do enjoy driving Doc."

The gift Danson purchased was a silver pin, part of a small selection on display in a cabinet in the Museum's foyer. This was one of the Museum's first sales of a new style of Hopi jewelry— Hopi overlay. Because of the pin's history, when Ned Danson became director, he bought the pin back from his sister and placed it in the Museum collection.

In the fall of 1940, instead of going to North Carolina, Danson's mother rented a house in Tucson only a few blocks from the Haury residence so that she and her son could live together during the school year. Before leaving Cincinnati, she sent her long-time maid Gertrude Carter to set the house up for her.

Ned reported to his mother that "Gertrude is busy getting the house in order . . . , putting away linen, polishing silver, and doing odds and ends." But he expressed concern that his mother had sent "no serving spoons out with the silver, no salad forks and only one silver serving fork. Are you bringing them? Otherwise everything is fine."

After her arrival, Ann Danson audited a few introductory classes in anthropology so she could understand the field that had become her son's passion. He recalled hearing her in their home practicing the names of the different Hopi mesas and villages. Following the family's tradition, Ned and his mother enjoyed giving parties, hosting both students and professors, one of whom ended up falling into a flower garden after enjoying a notoriously strong mint julep.

In the summer of 1941, Ned Danson was given approval to begin field work for his master's thesis. His assignment was an archaeological survey of the valley and hills surrounding the Santa Cruz River, which flowed south from the San Rafael Valley in southern Arizona into Mexico, then back north into Arizona. In a letter to his mother, he related the first day of the survey:

> Monday morning I loaded everything in the car, ice box, food, gasoline stove, gasoline, chair, wash basin, milk

can full of water, suitcase, map case, typewriter, etc. and
started off for the San Rafael Valley. . . . I found one site
and called it a day. Found a nice place to camp under
a hill in a park of live oaks. It was grand sleeping and
I was very comfortable in the station wagon on my air
mattress. . . . Wednesday I searched the bluffs on the
east side of the river and found [a] site. Then nothing
the rest of the morning. The country is quite extensive
there in the valley and I really need a horse. As it was,
my feet were killing me so after lunch I came on back
to the Ranch—a day early but without a horse I was
wasting my time and hurting my feet. Cowboy boots are
poor things to walk in.

Despite his love of driving, Danson found his wooden-body
Pontiac station wagon could not get to many areas of his survey.
And so, in order to take him where he wanted to go, he borrowed
a horse from his uncle and searched for sites on horseback.

As the survey progressed, he needed to ask permission to enter the property of the ranchers who owned land along the river.
"The ranchers were universally nice to me," he said, "not one was
disagreeable and all gave me permission—Lots of fun, really."

Working his way down the Santa Cruz, he identified numerous sites and collected prehistoric pottery sherds to help date the
sites. As he progressed, he started to see an unusual pattern that
would later be identified by archaeologists as "check dams."

I think the most interesting finds of that summer were
the large, late village sites through which or near which
ran wide, shallow rock lines or depressions. Some were
quite long, some short, but they were obviously not
drainage ditches, nor roads, nor made for defenses. I
called them race tracks and, as far as I know, no one has
yet made a definitive statement about them.

That August, Dr. Haury asked Danson to drive him on a month-long excursion around the American Southwest. Haury planned to take some of the first color photographs of important archaeological sites in the region, including Montezuma's Castle, Wupatki, Betatakin, Keet Seel, Canyon de Chelly and Mesa Verde. He was planning a special exhibit at the Arizona State Museum, focused on sites where he and others had collected samples of wooden beams whose rings had been analyzed and compared in order to establish a basic chronology of Southwestern prehistory. Development of that timeline had been one of the first achievements of the new science of tree-ring dating—dendrochronology.

On the trip, Danson discovered that driving was not to be his only duty. When leaving the car, he carried his mentor's camera, "a heavy, cumbersome affair that felt like it was determined to tear my arms out of their sockets. I don't think Emil used it again unless it was located in one spot."

"Why Emil asked me to go with him, I don't know," Danson later wrote, "but it gave me an interesting glimpse into the prehistory of the Southwest and an introduction to the men and women who were important in the excavations and in the writing of the prehistory of the area."

On Labor Day weekend, 1941, Danson drove to Balboa Island, California, to pick up his aunt, Florence Allen Sawyer, and take her to see his adopted state. When Ned arrived, he found that his aunt had an old Glendale friend around his age, Virginia "Jimmy" Coke, staying with her. And so, they would have to wait until Monday to begin their journey.

Jimmy invited Danson to a party at the home of her sister's La Jolla in-laws. At the party, she introduced Ned to a friend of hers from Pasadena, named Jessica Harriet MacMaster.

Jessica MacMaster had been born in Seattle, Washington, in the same year as Ned Danson. She spent her early years in Seattle and her summers at her great-grandparents' family compound, next to a golf course at Wing Point on Bainbridge Island

Jessica MacMaster, about 1940

in Puget Sound. In 1924, when she was about eight, the family moved to the Los Angeles area but continued to spend their summers at Wing Point.

Like Danson, Jessica's father was a British immigrant. In his case, James Eric MacMaster was a proud Scot. Although he grew up in London, he had been born in Minneapolis while his parents were on a business trip to America. Although bothered throughout his life that he had not been born in Britain, he returned to America at twenty-one, the same age E. B. Danson, Sr., had been when he immigrated to America in 1883. Initially intending to visit relatives, then return home, MacMaster attended Seattle's St. Paul's Episcopal Church with his uncle, met the rector's stepdaughter, Mary Lucile Johnston, and fell in love.

Jessica was the younger of the two MacMaster children. Her older sister, Eileen, was married to another British immigrant named Jeffrey Lungé. Lungé was an artist whose preferred subject matter was beaches, birds, and seascapes. Danson would later help change that.

That Monday, Danson drove his aunt to the Grand Canyon and shared with her the state he loved, visiting the Museum of Northern Arizona on the way. Then he returned to the university and the pursuit of his master's degree. Ned Danson, after a youth of physical and intellectual wandering, had a clear plan for his life. He had chosen a profession, and he owned one hundred acres of Kenyon Ranch, where he intended to build a small home for himself.

But the Imperial Japanese High Command had other plans.

Even before the attack on Pearl Harbor, tensions were rising, and America was mobilizing for war. In the lottery to determine draft order, Danson's number was very low, making it likely he would soon be drafted into the Army. But his easy way with making friends diverted him onto a different path. Shortly after he met Jessica MacMaster, two Naval officers vacationed at Kenyon Ranch. Danson had become so friendly with one, Captain Jim Lowry, and his wife Edith, that he had not only been invited to come visit them at their home in Coronado, California, but Lowry also gave him some advice about the coming war. After the conversation, Ned wrote to his mother, "It's hard to write this letter, especially when I know you want so much for me to finish my masters, but my dear—I'm afraid I won't be able to—for the draft has its long fingers on me, and I see no way of avoiding it."

"Archaeology isn't a war job," he concluded, "and it can wait a few more years. . . ." Captain Lowry suggested that Danson be commissioned as an Ensign in the Navy, warning him that he would not be in for a "cush" job. But with his background, particularly traveling on the *Yankee*, he could be useful.

Danson considered his advice. And, in January, 1942, he drew up his will and moved to California. Captain and Mrs. Lowry asked him to stay with them at their home in Coronado while waiting for his induction. The wait was longer than expected. As Danson later pieced together, a major reason for the delay was due to a lost document. As a part of the induction process, the Navy sent a form requesting information about Danson to the police chief of Tubac, Arizona. But the Navy didn't know that the last person in Tubac to hold the position of chief of police had been "an *alcalde*, the Spanish head of Tubac in the 1700s." The Postmistress eventually settled on giving the letter to a local border guard who passed by while she was trying to figure out where to deliver the envelope. But before he could open it, he spotted someone he suspected of crossing the border illegally and gave chase, losing the letter. Danson's induction papers finally arrived in San Diego on February 29, 1942. Despite the delay, Danson found the change sudden. "One day a civilian," he observed, "and the next an Ensign in the Navy."

The use the Navy found for a man who had sailed across the world, including six months in the South Pacific, was in communications—coding and receiving messages, then typing them and seeing that they were delivered. Although Danson felt that they did not use his skills to the utmost, he found the assignment interesting and readily adapted to his new role. He suspected that most of the senior officers thought communications dull. But already interested in history and in how organizations were run, he especially liked the opportunity to understand the big picture through the messages he handled. He recalled following the first naval battles between the United States and Japan as he would a baseball game being broadcast over the radio.

Ensign Danson was assigned to the Naval District headquarters in San Diego, under a superior officer named Bill Allen. This Bill Allen, whose formal name was Willis Allen, was not related to Danson, but their friendship would become close and prove mutually helpful later in the war. Danson's work was intense, the shifts long. Due to the sensitivity of his job, he had to keep track of his movements precisely and account for every code book at the end of each shift. Despite all the time and energy devoted to his job, he still had time to become known by his colleagues as "Ensign Danson the Dancin' Ensign."

One weekend in 1942, Jessica MacMaster called to say she would be staying at the Hotel Del Coronado with a friend of hers from Pasadena. Jessica had a date with the friend's brother. She suggested that Ned make it a double date by going out with her friend.

Danson went to the Hotel Del Coronado and waited in the lobby for the two women. He later wrote that he would "never forget sitting in the huge wonderful old room and watching the elevator come down into the lobby. The elevator was made of open wire scrolls, and I could see Jessica coming down. She had on a black silk dress printed with great flaming hibiscus flowers and green leaves. She was gorgeous and knocked me out." Jessica's friend and her brother ended up sitting in the back seat of the car while Ned Danson and Jessica MacMaster talked the entire time in the front.

During the evening, Danson told Jessica, "You're going to love Arizona."

Jessica recalled thinking, *Wow, what a line!*

Soon after, Danson wrote to his mother.

She certainly is a peach Mother, and I'm really sure. I didn't ever feel this way about Tinker—I miss her all the time she is gone, and plan for her next visit as soon as she goes. I plan our home on the Ranch—and the jewels I am going to get for her—my only worry is about Jess and Arizona. Will she like it and will she like going on expeditions and really roughing it. She has "camped out" and liked it, but never "lived out." There's a big, big difference. But she loves the open, is a good sport, has imagination and intelligent interest, all necessary attributes for a person who likes to live in the rough. Also a sense of humor, which she has. . . . Now I'll answer any questions I can. . . . Yes of course tell Ann that I'm in love—not engaged but doing my darndest to be.

That year, Danson dated Jessica MacMaster periodically when she came down to San Diego or he drove up to Pasadena. Just a year after Ned and Jessica met, in September, Ned took Jessica's father for lunch to ask for his daughter's hand in marriage. Later that day, Ned proposed to Jessica on the beach in La Jolla, giving her his mother's and maternal grandmother's diamond in a new ring setting he had designed. Ensign Edward B. Danson and Jessica MacMaster were married on November 7, 1942, in Pasadena's All Saints Episcopal Church.

The newly married Dansons spent their honeymoon at Lake Arrowhead, and then Danson went back to work. Housing was limited in San Diego, so Jessica and Ned shared an apartment with Ned's former roommates for a few days until they could find their own place. Ned and Jessica celebrated their first Christmas in their rented Coronado apartment with a small tree and the Danson family's traditional large Christmas stockings.

While stationed in San Diego, Danson became senior watch officer and was promoted to Lieutenant Junior Grade. When

Jessica and Ned honeymooning at Lake Arrowhead, California, 1942

The Dansons' first Christmas, Coronado, California

one of his friends volunteered to go to the Pacific as a part of an intelligence group that would provide information to those landing on the islands, Danson decided he wanted to go as well. He discussed the matter with Jessica and then volunteered. He later considered that a mistake. He was turned down by the intelligence group, only to receive orders to ship out as a communications officer with one of the Joint Army-Navy Communications groups that would do the actual landing itself. "I learned a lesson that day," Danson wrote. "Never apply for one job. It only attracts attention to your name and you don't usually get the job you want."

He sold his woodie station wagon to the Navy for war use, leaving a 1936 Ford coupe for Jessica, and, on June 6, 1943, shipped out for New Caledonia. After less than a decade, he would be back in the South Pacific. He traveled to his new post on a luxury liner that had been converted into a troop transport. The ship's food, he reported, was still excellent.

He left a wife not merely worried for her husband's safety, but pregnant as well with their first child. Jessica moved back to live next door to her parents in Pasadena, where her father was serving in the British Consular Service in Los Angeles.

While Jessica Danson stayed busy producing the next generation, Lt. Danson continued with the war effort. He was first stationed on New Caledonia at a base outside of Noumea. He found the experience boring. The base had been established and then forgotten. There was no enemy. There were no orders. Danson abhorred boredom.

While on leave in Noumea, Danson found that the Admiral's communications center was run by Willis Allen. He went to meet his friend and told him he had nothing to do where he was. Allen wanted Ned to work for him again, but Danson felt honor-bound to ask his commanding officer for approval. At first it was denied, but later Danson was approved to work a regular shift under Allen for two months, returning to his official camp only once a week to report in. After work each day, he and Willis Allen went to the officer's club to drink and play the slot machine and watch movies.

Although he was on leave from his anthropological studies, his interest remained. When he and a fellow officer were given a weekend leave, they borrowed a jeep and drove across New Caledonia to see what they could find. On the journey, they came upon an empty village. One of the huts in the village had a tall, conical roof. Danson realized that it was a primitive religious building, and its presence was a sign the missionaries had not yet replaced all of the island's native religion. Interested both in the anthropological subtext and the aesthetics, Danson drew a detailed sketch of the hut and sent it to his family.

Danson sent other anthropological reports and sketches to Emil Haury. He was only one of several of Haury's students, serving in the war, who gave their professor similar descriptions of life in the far-flung places to which they had been assigned.

In late October 1943, Lt. Danson was reassigned. He was to participate in the invasion of Bougainville, one of the Solomon Islands, to land with the second wave of U.S. Marines. On November 2, his wife's birthday, Danson found himself on a troop ship within sight of islands he had visited during his *Yankee* voyage, waiting for the ship's bow ramp to open.

The scene was chaotic. The landing craft's pilot missed his mark, and Danson stepped off the ramp, only to sink into the water. His struggle onto the beach was far from secure, and he joined numerous marines and other sailors in dodging bullets and explosions as they raced from the water to the trees, which themselves provided little safety. Danson recalled seeing another American shooting at a tree under which he himself had passed only a few minutes before. A Japanese soldier fell from the canopy. Danson had no idea why he had escaped being shot dead.

Later, the Lieutenant wrote about his experiences on Bougainville to his mother, his wife and to his older sister, Virginia. His letters to his wife and mother told about what he had to eat, what hours he worked and even included a drawing of the floor plan of his tent, showing where he kept his books, family photographs, and the box containing his supply of caviar and other treasures.

His letters to his sister told the full truth. Although unable to give details about his location, he did tell her:

> It really was something the first day here and believe me I never want to go through another. Not that I was in any more danger than anyone else, but after being dumped in the water and rolled head over heels with my pack, gun, helmet, and everything, and then having to walk over a mile through thick sand with my pack. . . . Well I was a plenty tired fellow that night. For over a week, I didn't change clothes, and when we at last got down here where we could get a bath, believe me it felt wonderful. . . .

But, ever the lover of beauty, he added, "This is a pretty island with a big volcano back of us and south a bit which smokes all day long and at night glows red against the sky. North of us are two very high peaks and behind us a low flat mountain." That was the land the Japanese held, while for weeks the Americans were confined to territory along the shore that was "mostly low and flat with some coconut plantations and lots of swampy jungle. . . . Couldn't even dig a decent foxhole."

At the beginning, Ned Danson and one other officer ran all American military communications on Bougainville.

> It was a hard and important job. I remember one night, when I was the voice directing shell fire from destroyers who were laying down a barrage of shells in front of an advancing Marine force trying to take a high rise on the flank of the area we held. The Captain would ask for shelling, the destroyer would fire, our trailer would shake, the Captain would yell "Higher" or "50 yards further." I'd send the message, another round would be

Dive bomber landing on Bougainville Island

Danson (front) in Bougainville Communications Center, 1944

Officers' Mess, Bougainville Island (Danson at far left), 1944

heard landing, another shake. . . . Gradually, the attack
succeeded and the high hill on our flank was taken so
we didn't get shelled from that area any more. I felt I was
doing something to really help.

In the following weeks, the chaos Danson hid from his wife
and mother slowly retreated, the terrain eventually becoming secure enough for American forces to build an airfield. But danger
from the Japanese could still flare up at a moment's notice.

Another real danger came from Danson's Captain. He considered the Captain a poor leader, or in his words, "a dud." Danson's team ran communications twenty-four hours a day from a
"dugout"—a shelter similar to half-buried "pit-houses" used by
several of the prehistoric Southwest cultures he had studied. If a
shell landed near the dugout, the team risked being killed, and
the only line of communications off the island would have been
severed. The sole protection they had from shrapnel was a triple-
thick wall of sandbags.

Danson was horrified one day, when he returned from getting
the mail, to see junior officers removing sandbags from around
the communications dugout and placing them around the Captain's tent, making quarters for one person more secure while
risking the lives of many. This went against the values he had
learned from his father, who had given money to people in need,
and against the leadership skills that he had learned from Irving
Johnson and Emil Haury, who looked after those under them.

When Danson objected to the Captain's orders, the Captain
simply responded that more sandbags were due to come in the
next day. The Captain said he would send the old bags back to
the communications tent, keeping the fresh ones for himself.
Danson replied that, without the protection the sandbags offered, if there were any shelling, he would order his men to leave
their communications tent and find the closest foxhole.

The Captain's trust in military supply lines proved to be too
strong. The new sandbags took eleven days to be delivered. Dur-

ing that time, the communications staff had to spend up to six hours each day in their foxholes.

With communication on so vital an island under threat, a mere four days after the problem started, the Navy sent a lieutenant from San Francisco to the Operational Command Center in New Caledonia to find out what was going on.

The lieutenant spoke to Willis Allen, who said Ned Danson was the man he needed to talk to in order to understand the situation. The lieutenant flew to Bougainville to see him.

The discredited captain was replaced by another captain who corrected the errors of his predecessor. Communications then began to flow smoothly. Danson's ability to work hard and win friends had saved his company and maybe much more.

But there were still surprises. "One night on duty," Danson wrote, "the door bell rang (our doors were heavily locked). When I opened the door, an exhausted sweating man staggered in. He had said the correct password, but I was startled for he looked quite Japanese." The man turned out to be Navajo. He was one of the Code Talkers, Navajo servicemen who used their own language as the basis for a complex code that the Japanese were never able to break. Upon further conversation, Danson learned that he was "from up near Chinle," in Arizona, and that, "He had been shot at by our own marines in their foxholes, who thought he was a part of a Japanese offensive! We had coffee and talked."

That was not the only connection to his past that Danson found on Bougainville. As the island became safer, he came to know more of the American forces and discovered that one of the doctors on the island had married a woman who had sailed with him on the first voyage of the *Yankee*.

Now that the young lieutenant could focus on more than survival and his duties, he was given an opportunity to display the sense of style that led the *Yankee* crewmembers to call him "The Duke." Before Christmas, when he went to pick up the mail for the company, he found a package waiting for him containing twelve sets of sterling silver dinner knives and forks and five Chantilly silver tea spoons. They had been ordered by his mother as a present for the family and were supposed to have been shipped to Jessica in Pasadena. By mistake, they ended up in a war zone. His initial instinct was to set up a "splendid mess" for his fellow officers, but he thought better of the idea and sent them to Jessica.

While things were settling down in Bougainville, in Pasadena, Jessica's due date was fast approaching. Hoping not just for a grandchild but a grandson, Ann Allen Danson purchased a war bond in the name of "Edward Bridge Danson III" and waited. The child was born on January 11, 1944, with Jessica's sister, Eileen, performing the traditional father's role of anxiously pacing in the waiting room until the birth was announced.

War bonds held no mystical power over procreation. The child was a girl. Lieutenant Danson received word of the birth of his daughter, Jessica Ann Danson, or Jan, two weeks after she was born.

By then, Danson was serving as head of the officers' mess and had been assigned to oversee the building of an officers' club while still carrying out his responsibilities in communications. But his life was still in danger. While he and others were waiting on the beach to pick up supplies from a landing craft, they heard a shell screaming towards them. Danson ran one way. A man standing next to him ran in another direction and the next moment was killed.

By April, however, Bougainville Island was secure. Without a constant threat to his life or heavy communications traffic, Danson faced another, subtler problem. "I think this is the worst part of war," he wrote to his sister, "boredom. When the fight's really going on, you're too tired and filthy, hot and mad to be bored, or worried. But now there is a sense of waiting—a slow dying away of all purpose—and a deadly monotony."

Much as he had always hated boredom, as the weeks drew on, there were signs he had a larger problem. He began to lose weight rapidly and was increasingly nervous. A doctor examined him and recommended that he be sent to a hospital behind the lines for rest and relaxation, followed by reassignment elsewhere.

"That was OK with me," Danson later wrote. After seven months on Bougainville, with the main action over and the crisis in communications resolved, he felt he had done what he could for the war effort.

A few weeks later, Jessica received a phone call from Ned's former commanding officer, telling her of his hospitalization. Jessica reported the message to her mother-in-law, saying that the commander had added:

> Ned was magnificent in the landing, that actually they couldn't have got along without him. And his efficiency was grand. When the senior officer gave out Ned carried on with flying colors, and that the two commanding officers were very fond of him, in fact he was the only one that got along with them. Also several marvelous letters of commendation had been written about him, and his fitness report was wonderful (a fitness report concerns your personality & character and how you react in a crisis).

Danson, now a full lieutenant, was diagnosed with battle fatigue. He spent several weeks recuperating in a hospital on Espiritu Santo Island in the New Hebrides, an island he had visited on his *Yankee* voyage. His weight would eventually return to normal and his nerves calm. But one medical condition that would have long lasting consequences involved his teeth. A Navy dentist had performed shoddy work on Danson. Although Ned left the South Pacific with his teeth intact, that would not last.

After six weeks in medical wards, he was shipped home to a Naval hospital in Oakland, California. "The highest spot of the whole trip," Danson said in a letter to his mother, "[was] when we sailed under the Golden Gate Bridge in the early morning.

How the boys did yell! That bridge has assumed the same place in our thoughts as the Statue of Liberty—home!!"

From Oakland, Danson was transferred to the Naval Rest Home in Rancho Santa Fe near San Diego to recuperate. On weekends he was allowed to visit Jessica in Pasadena, and there he finally met his daughter. On those weekends, Ned Danson not only got used to being a father but came to understand a key aspect of his wife's personality.

During one of those weekend visits, Ned came down to join Jessica's family for a meal. He looked across the table to his brother-in-law, Jeffrey Lungé, and recognized something at once.

"That's my jacket," he said to Jeffrey, who was wearing Ned's favorite sport jacket. Jessica explained to her husband that she had given the jacket to Jeffrey months before.

When Ned inquired as to why, she replied, "You hadn't been wearing it." This was one of his wife's key traits, her almost saintly need to give. Sometimes, to give more than she should. Frustrating as Danson sometimes found it, this trait would be a great boon later in his career.

Another clash in style between Jessica and Ned was made apparent on birthdays and Christmases. The frugal MacMaster had married into a family that sent piles of presents to one another. Before Christmas, Ned's mother and sisters would send presents wrapped in red tissue paper and marked from "Santa" to fill the traditional leg-length yuletide stockings to the brim. Jessica felt she could never compete. But while Ned Danson lived to receive presents, he was just as eager to give them, sometimes giving gifts to others on his own birthday.

After Danson had recovered enough to return to active duty, he again worked in communications in San Diego. But after a couple of months, he received orders to report to Washington, D.C., for further training in communications for the planned invasion of Japan. Once more, Danson left his wife and daughter and headed east. He missed a second Christmas with his wife and his daughter's first one.

Meeting Jan for the first time, fall 1944

He found a room to rent in the Washington house belonging to Major General Walton Walker. Danson loved the experience. Not only did he find it a pleasant place to stay, but he also enjoyed meeting Mrs. Walker's close friends Mrs. George Patton and Mrs. Dwight D. Eisenhower.

When her friends visited, Mrs. Walker often asked him, "Ned, would you be our butler?" So he became their regular bartender, serving wives of high-ranking officers and even being allowed to have a few drinks with them. While in Washington, Danson also was able to reconnect with friends from Cincinnati, Cornell and Arizona who were passing through or stationed in the area.

He also spent some of his free time at museums. Upon visiting the National Portrait Gallery, he proclaimed that it was a "really impressive and beautiful place. The collections of paintings are wonderful." And as the grandson of an architect, he added that the building itself was "perfect." The anthropological collections at the Smithsonian received a more nuanced evaluation. "They have huge quantities of stuff," he wrote to his sister. But he added, with a critical eye he would one day put to use in his own museum, "mostly all [their artifacts are] poorly exhibited."

"Washington was a vital busy place," he wrote "and if one were ambitious, the place to be. But I wasn't ambitious. I wanted to get back home." After two months, Danson was ordered back to California to head an amphibious communications group, which, he later learned, would have been part of the initial surge during the invasion of Japan.

When Danson returned to San Diego to await further orders, Jessica and Jan joined him in a rented house on a hill overlooking the San Diego airport and harbor. In early August, Ned and Jessica joined friends to take a quick vacation at Lake Arrowhead. One of the friends was a physicist, and, on the drive home, when they heard radio reports of the atomic bombing of Hiroshima, he was able to explain the significance of the event.

That night, the Dansons met with Jimmy, the woman who had introduced them, and her husband, Charlie Robinson. Jimmy had been working as a secretary for a number of California Institute of Technology atomic scientists, and her husband was a postgraduate student with an understanding of atomic energy. The conversation naturally focused on the bombing.

"I know Charlie had a fairly low opinion of [me]. . . ," Danson recalled, "but it changed that night as I would toss into the conversation words such as 'fission' and 'fusion,' 'amounts of energy,' etc." It was another example of Danson using his social skills and intellect to win someone over.

A few days later, Japan surrendered, freeing Lieutenant Danson from what may well have been a suicide mission. Ned, Jessica and Jan joined in the San Diego festivities celebrating the end of the war. Then Ned Danson shifted his focus from war and the Navy back to Arizona.

There was no more need to be part of the war business. Anthropology beckoned.

Ned and Jessica with Peg Hurley (center) sailing on Lake Arrowhead, 1944

By Thanksgiving of 1945, Ned Danson was back in Arizona and had spoken with Emil Haury about resuming his studies in anthropology. Rather than building a house at Kenyon Ranch, as Danson had once intended, the family bought a home in Tucson a few blocks from the Haurys. He took classes to refresh his knowledge and wrote up reports of the work he had done before the war. When he felt ready, with Haury's support, Danson decided to apply for a doctoral program in anthropology.

This, however, was something the University of Arizona did not yet offer, so it was time for the man who had made himself a Westerner to head east once more. At Haury's suggestion, Ned Danson applied to enter the graduate program at Harvard University.

In the spring of 1946, before receiving an answer, he drove east. Jessica and Jan traveled with him as far as Cincinnati and stayed there with Danson's relatives. He left the car there and flew on to Massachusetts.

At that time, the head of Harvard's Department of Anthropology was Dr. Earnest Hooton. Danson arranged a meeting and asked the professor if he had been accepted, adding that he had flown in to hear the answer.

"You flew in?" Dr. Hooton asked, flying for business not being as common as in later decades.

"Yes, sir," Danson replied.

Dr. Hooton was so impressed with this bold act that he said, "Yes, of course you are." The man who hadn't finished high school was now going to attend one of the world's most prestigious universities.

Ned Danson spent the summer before his first term at Harvard at the University of Arizona's new Archaeological Field School at Point of Pines on the San Carlos Apache Indian Reservation in east-central Arizona. The land around Point of Pines was rich in prehistory, but the students and staff, under the leadership of Emil Haury, spent almost as much time helping to build the new camp as they did digging up artifacts from the past. Like Danson, most of the other students had delayed their studies because of the war. He reported that, as a result, they "played hard and worked hard. I would say we even drank hard." Danson had asked Haury if he could bring a bottle of bourbon with him to the officially "dry" reservation, and, receiving his permission, brought several. Almost every night at the field school there was a cocktail party in someone's tent, and Danson found the comity healing.

A month later, in the fall of 1946, the Dansons moved to Cambridge, Massachusetts. Jessica was thrilled to be in New England for the first time in her life, and the small family settled into a two-room apartment at the Continental Hotel. Jan was given the bedroom, while Ned and Jessica slept in the living room.

Danson's professor and mentor at Harvard was Jo Brew, whom he had first met at Awat'ovi before the war. Brew was Curator of North American Archaeology at Harvard's Peabody Museum of Archaeology, one of the oldest museums in the world dedicated to anthropology. For Danson's dissertation,

Point of Pines crew, 1946. (Top row, left to right) Kepler Lewis, Jim Hall, Tom Onstott, Carl Huffaker, Rex Gerald, Ned Danson (Center row) Carl Larsen, Ted Stearns, Hulda Haury, Sarge Brown (Front row) Emil Haury, Gladys Sayles, Loren Haury, Allan Haury, Tom Caine, Manice Lockwood, Arnold Withers

Brew suggested that he survey the Upper Gila River basin, an area of 14,500 square miles of wilderness along the Arizona-New Mexico border.

At the time, that part of the American Southwest had not been developed, and much of it had not been visited by archaeologists. Most of it was cattle country, crisscrossed with dirt roads. Watson Smith, a Peabody Museum archaeologist Ned became close to at Harvard, later described Catron County, a major part of Danson's survey area, as being "notable for not having more things than any other county in the United States. It had no telephone, no telegraph, no railroad, no water system, no electric lighting; it had no hospital, two schools—and there were a good many other things that it didn't have." As with the adventurers in the books of his youth, Danson's task was to go out into the wilderness to survey the area, driving the poor, often muddy roads, walking the hills and valleys, cataloguing the existence of visible prehistoric pueblos or looking for more

Map of Ned Danson's doctoral survey area (top). Mariana Mesa, New Mexico, part of survey area (above)

Ned and Jeffrey Lungé at Kendall's cabin, Nutrioso, Arizona, 1947

subtle signs where pithouses or religious structures might be buried. He planned to collect samples of pot sherds at each site; their designs, typical of different prehistoric periods, would help him date the sites. Over three summers, Danson would fill in a map that had been, archaeologically, blank.

The location picked for his survey placed Danson in the middle of an academic conflict between his two mentors, Haury and Brew. Although they were close friends, they strongly disagreed over Haury's concept of a distinct "Mogollon Culture." The Mogollon was a group of mountain people living in eastern Arizona and western New Mexico from the 2nd to the 15th century. Haury argued that their way of life differed enough from that of the surrounding peoples for them to be considered a separate culture, while Brew sided with those who considered the Mogollon to be best described as a sub-culture of the Ancestral Pueblo of the Colorado Plateau. Danson used his diplomatic skills to find a way not to antagonize either of his mentors. His final dissertation noted that the culture he had studied met all the definitions for Haury's Mogollon without declaring whether Danson approved of the definition or not.

In the summer of 1947, after a school year filled with anthropology classes with some of the great professors of the time, Danson began the survey of the Upper Gila River basin by driving his car over 6,500 miles to get to know the area.

Brew visited his student several times during the survey. During one visit, the two men took time off to travel to Point of Pines, where Emil Haury was again running the University of Arizona's summer field school. As always, Danson made friends quickly. Two of the people at the field school, Raymond "Ray" Thompson, an undergraduate, and Molly Kendall, a member of a Southern Arizona ranching family, who was employed by the Arizona State Museum, became his friends. Their friendship grew closer the next year when Ray Thompson joined Danson as a student at Harvard. In 1948, barely a year and a half after first meeting the two, Ned Danson served as the best man at their wedding.

The same summer Danson began his survey, Jessica and their daughter returned to California to live near her parents in Coronado. Jessica was pregnant with the Danson's second child, and Ned felt he could not possibly complete his studies while living in a one-bedroom apartment with a baby and a four-year-old.

But after months alone, working in the field and taking classes, he made sure to spend his Christmas break with his family in Coronado. Therefore, he was present when, on December 29, 1947, the child for whom Ann Allen Danson had bought the war bond, Edward Bridge Danson III—Ted—was finally born.

It was not just the matriarch of the Danson family who had wanted a boy. Already the grandfather of three girls, James Eric MacMaster, who had gone lame years earlier, ran up the stairs of the family home to report that he at last had a grandson. When Jessica heard this, she responded with, "What's wrong with little girls?"

During the summers when he was doing field work, Ned was able to visit his family only briefly. The two MacMaster sisters, Jessica and Eileen, had always been close. And now, with both of them wives and mothers, they started a tradition of spending part of each summer together.

While the two sisters were enjoying Coronado, Danson invited Eileen's husband, Jeffrey Lungé, to join him in 1948 for a few weeks vacation at his survey base in eastern Arizona. Jeffrey took the train from Pasadena to Holbrook. Ned met him at the station, and they drove to the log cabin near the town of Nutrioso that Molly Kendall's father had allowed him to use as his field headquarters. The trip, passing through the multi-colored splendor of the Painted Desert, introduced Jeffrey Lungé to Arizona.

While Danson searched for sites, his brother-in-law painted and sketched the landscapes. Thanks to Danson, Arizona had a new lover. Lungé, an artist who had focused on painting seascapes for years, started to add Southwestern themes to his repertoire. That year, he produced a painting of Ned's base of operations that hung in Ned and Jessica's homes for the rest of their lives.

Jess, Ted, Ned and Jan Danson, 1948

With his class work finished, but with more work needed before he could write up the results of his survey and earn his Ph.D., Danson returned to his family in Coronado in the fall of 1949. While there, he received a telephone call from his old University of Arizona classmate, Arnie Withers, now an anthropology professor at the University of Denver. Withers had heard about a professorship opening at the University of Colorado in Boulder. They needed someone who could teach courses in beginning anthropology, Southwestern American archaeology, and, in an important sign of Danson's future career, museum studies. Withers had recommended Danson to the department head. Danson consulted with Emil Haury about taking a professorship before completing his doctorate. Haury wrote back, "My first and immediate reaction is that by all means accept the Boulder offer. . . . The connection with the University of Colorado would be a feather in your cap. An important issue involved is proving that you can teach."

Ned discussed the opportunity with Jessica, and within a week flew to the University to be interviewed. They offered him the job. Danson bought a house, a "cute little stone Swiss

Chalet . . . " at the foot of "the majestic Flat Iron Mountains of
the Front Range."

The family arrived in Boulder on New Years Day, 1949,
during a blizzard. Danson drove the last few miles with his head
out the window in order to see the road. The next day Jan and
Jessica looked out the front door and saw skiers heading straight
towards their house. The ski run, which had been invisible the
day before, stopped just across the road from their home.

Soon after their arrival, Danson began teaching anthropology classes for the first time. He recalled that he enjoyed himself
in Boulder, especially his interactions with new colleagues. And
the Dansons had an active social life. The head of the University's art department, Alden Megrew, lived with his wife Rue two
doors down the street. The Megrews became close friends with
Ned and Jessica and introduced them to other members of the
University, including a number of artists. "We were young and
full of energy," Danson recalled, "and soon we were caught up
in a social whirl which was headed by Bob and Amy Stearns. He
was then the President of the University and a brilliant and lik-
able person. Years later Bob and I served on the National Parks
Advisory Board together."

While Danson enjoyed teaching, he did have one problem.
He felt he was "expected to become excited by Plains archaeology." But he never did. "The Southwest was always my cup of tea."

Fortunately, his dissertation work kept him connected with
the Southwest. In 1949, Danson spent a third summer doing
field work, this time near Quemado, New Mexico, while Jessica, Jan and Ted stayed with Jessica's parents in California. He
made his camp at the Peabody Museum's field school, run by
Watson Smith, with a crew that included Danson's fellow Harvard graduate student Raymond Thompson and his new bride,
Molly. Over the season, Smith, joining Haury and Brew, became
the third of Danson's great anthropological mentors.

Watson Smith was also from a well-to-do Cincinnati family, though he and Danson had never met in their home town.

Ned, Ted, and Patches outside Boulder home, 1949

Boulder living room designed by Ned Danson, 1950

Members of the Peabody Museum selected Smith's site, based on the survey work Danson had done over the past few summers. "Contacts had already been made by Ned with many of the residents of the area, with whom he had been acquainted," Smith wrote, "and because he was a friendly and gregarious man, he had broken the ice for us. . . ." Smith was impressed by Danson—his style as much as his intellect. In his autobiography, Smith wrote:

> Ned Danson . . . stands as my criterion of sartorial elegance. . . . I think it is quaintly odd to recall that Ned could descend into a dusty trench, garbed in Bond Street elegance, wield a shovel, extract a buried artifact, and rise again as immaculate as Venus on her shell. It was a *tour-de-beche* that some of the students, in dank dungarees, mud-grimed and sweating, found difficult to forgive.

Following his summer in the field, the Danson family gathered again in Colorado. Their Boulder home was small and Ned, following in his father's and paternal grandfather's footsteps, designed an addition to the house. The addition was completed in 1950.

In Boulder, the Danson family adopted a three-year old dog, called Patches because of the brown and black splotches covering her body. Adopted when Ted was one-and-a-half, Patches became particularly close to the young boy. On her first evening with the family, she and Ted chased each other around the living room until they finally knocked over a lamp. Later, when Patches went into heat, Danson took an intense dislike to one of her suitors. After verbally trying to keep the suitor from sneaking up the back steps and into the house where Patches was locked up, Danson picked up a broom and swung hard. He hit the clothes line, and the broom bounced back and hit him on the head, instead. In the end, Patches ended up having puppies, which fascinated the children.

Watson Smith, 1948

Danson, Stoudt, Ray and Molly Thompson, Watson Smith and J. O. Brew excavating Site 494, Mariana Mesa, summer 1949

Ned's home and office at the Peabody Museum Field Camp, summer 1949

With the field work for his dissertation complete, Danson spent the summer of 1950 in Boulder, analyzing his data, while Jessica and the children made their usual trip to California. Using the results from his survey, he co-wrote an article on the Casa Malpais archaeological site near Springerville, Arizona, that was printed in *Plateau*, a journal published by the Museum of Northern Arizona. While his family was still in California, Danson received a call from the University of Arizona. It was Harry Getty, who was acting head of the Department of Anthropology while Emil Haury was away on sabbatical. A position had opened in the department, and they wanted Ned Danson.

"When he said these magic words, 'Would I be interested in teaching at the University of Arizona?' I was struck dumb. But not so dumb that I couldn't say 'YES,' of course I'd like to teach at the University. Yes, I could come down to Tucson to take care of the business details. I couldn't believe my ears. I called Jessica, and she approved."

That summer, Ned and Jessica made a trip to Tucson to buy a house. The search for a new home was difficult, with Jessica disturbed to the point of tears when one of the prospects proved to be a former tuberculosis sanitarium. But they eventually found a house on five acres of desert in the Catalina Foothills, which was then the sparsely populated northern edge of town.

Danson recalled the first time they saw the house.

> The afternoon rain storms had come and it was getting dark. . . . As soon as we turned into the drive we knew it was right. The big old pepper tree had branches almost to the ground. The house was "L" shaped, had a flat roof and a porch looking out into the shady garden. There were fruit trees on the east side of the garden, big picture windows looking north from the living room, a big fireplace and three bedrooms and two baths.

With few houses nearby, the family would be able to look out on the desert or go for a quick desert walk whenever they

The Dansons' Tucson home, early 1950s

wished. They signed the papers, and Danson began to design a dining room where the garage had been.

In the fall, Ned drove his family from California to their new Tucson home. The journey was a trial.

> After having our lunch at the wharf in downtown San Diego, [we] drove on over the mountains. It was so hot as we drove into the desert that my arm had welts on it from touching the metal door handle inside the car. Jan demanded water and made her classic statement, "And the only reason we're going to Tucson is because he wants to work for THAT MAN!!" She meant, of course, her future father-in-law Emil Haury. . . . Ted, in Jess's arms, said once, "I'm hot. . . ." When we got to Yuma at 8:00 p.m., the temperature on the outdoor thermometer registered 128 degrees and Jess was suffering from heat exhaustion.

The University of Arizona had changed since Danson had left. Instead of an anthropology department with fifty students, by the mid 1950s, there were at least four hundred.

In his first year as a University of Arizona professor, Danson served as an assistant to Emil Haury, teaching Southwest

Archaeology. He also taught a course on museum methods. And just as Haury had taken an interest in him, Danson began to take an interest in his students. He did more than mentor good students. At one point, he discovered that a student had cheated on the final exam.

> After the class, the man came to the lecture platform and asked me what I was going to do. . . . I asked him if he were planning to take Anthro. I-B. He said, "No. . . ." Then I told him what I was going to do. . . . I said that if he would take Anthro. I-B, and if he got a B grade or better . . . I would give him credit for the year and hold his grade the first semester as an incomplete. He agreed, and at the end of second semester his grade average was A-. Years later, he stopped me on the street in Phoenix and told me that I had really changed his life, and thanked me.

One lecture Danson hoped would change the lives of many of his students stemmed from a mistake he had made in an earlier class. He had been talking about disadvantaged groups and mistakenly said that they should be "tolerated." A student came up to him after class and asked if "toleration" was the right word. Danson not only acknowledged his mistake at the next class, but took the opportunity to make a firm statement on how he believed people should treat others. He stated that "toleration" of others was not acceptable, as it suggested that the person doing the tolerating was in an inherently superior position, looking down on the other person. To illustrate his point, Danson climbed onto his desk and delivered his lecture as if looking down on a hypothetical person in front of him. It was a striking declaration of principles—principles that few, including Danson, could ever fully live up to.

Danson also believed it was important to give students a taste of work in the field. As Emil Haury had, he took students into the countryside during vacations and between semesters. On one trip, he brought them to Flagstaff where they stayed at the Museum of Northern Arizona's Research Center. "The trips were fun," Danson wrote, "and the students got to see areas and particular sites that made Southwestern archaeology easier to understand. It came alive for them."

In between fulfilling his duties as professor and father, Danson continued his quest for a Ph.D. He spent the summer of 1951 in Flagstaff, in Blue Jay, a cottage owned by the director of the Museum of Northern Arizona, Dr. Harold Sellers Colton and his wife, Mary-Russell Ferrell Colton. Each weekday, Danson left his home near the Coltons' house and retreated to a converted barn to work on his dissertation. As he wrote, Jessica spent the day in Blue Jay typing what he had written the day before. At night they both edited what Jessica had typed that day. Ted and Jan played in the pine woods with the Coltons' grandchildren. After seeing the Flagstaff All Indian Pow-Wow dances over the Fourth of July weekend, Jan decided she wanted to be an Apache maiden with long black hair.

The proximity of the cottage to the Colton's home provided opportunities for the two families to spend time together. Dr. Colton came from a patrician Pennsylvania family, similar in many ways to Danson's own, and Danson had an affinity for the Coltons' son, Ferrell, a sailor with whom he could share his experiences on the *Yankee*.

The mixed Flagstaff community of researchers, storekeepers, ranchers and Native Americans created a unique atmosphere. Although new to this community, when Danson saw smoke billowing up from a wildfire north of the Museum, he felt it was his duty to help. After first grabbing the pages of his dissertation and locking them up in the Museum's fire-proof safe, he and a colleague went as volunteers to help fight the fire. Their efforts lasted though the night, and the fire never came close to the Museum. Weeks later, Danson was surprised to receive a check from the Forest Service, paying him for what he thought was volunteer work.

In the fall, Danson returned to teaching in Tucson and completed his dissertation. In the spring of 1952, he traveled to Harvard University for his thesis defense. It was a success, and he received a document in Latin reading *"Edvardum* Bridge Danson." He had become "Dr. Danson" and, for the first time, felt free to refer to Dr. Haury as "Emil."

Once he completed the work for his Ph.D., and, with Jessica's help, rewrote it for publication by the Peabody Museum Press in 1957, Danson researched and published little, even though doing both was the standard path for advancement at a university. He preferred teaching and mentoring students. As had been the case earlier in his life, Danson pursued what interested him.

When not in the field, Danson spent his days living the comfortable life of a professor and family man. His days began with the cooing of doves in the desert and the chirping of sparrows in the garden.

Most mornings, Ned and Jessica shared coffee in bed before getting up for breakfast, discussing their plans for the day. Jan and Ted often came into their room and slipped into their bed to join the conversation. After breakfast in the dining room he had designed, he left for the University, and Jessica took Jan and Ted to school.

As soon as Ned returned home, he took off his shirt and tie, showered, put on a clean, pressed dress shirt and a fresh tie, then joined Jessica for a drink, while the children finished their dinner.

On weekends, Danson loved to work in the garden, tending his flowers, often hiring graduate students to assist him. The family attended church services on Sundays and mid-week at St. Philip's-in-the-Hills Episcopal Church, a building filled with art treasures from the Kress family collection, some of which Danson would later borrow for an exhibit at the University. In the evenings, he sometimes joined Jessica and the children on desert walks around their home.

The rest of the family shared Danson's love of reading. Even as his children grew older, he read to the whole family before bedtime. The stories he loved to read out loud ranged from Dr. Seuss books to the adventure stories he had enjoyed as a boy. Favorites the children later remembered hearing their father read included *Andivius Hedulio*, about a nobleman in the Roman Empire, and *The White House Gang*, the story of Teddy Roosevelt's son Quentin and his adventures in the White House with his elementary school friends.

Although the family had a metal swing set on their property, the children rarely used it as a swing but as the internal structure for forts they built. They preferred using the rope swing that hung from the old pepper tree.

The swing set fort proved to be a health hazard for young Ted, who fell off, cutting his head, one of several head injuries he suffered as a youth. But Ted suffered a greater health problem when he was four years old. He developed what doctors called "pre-rheumatic fever," and was forced to stay in bed for nine months. During that period, Jessica read to him most of the children's classics like *Treasure Island* and *Tom Sawyer*.

After recovering from his long illness, Ted developed a passion for horseback riding. Ned Danson took his son to a riding stable next to Tucson's Rillito racetrack, where one could rent horses for trail rides in the foothills. Jan preferred to play in the desert with several other girls her age. One of her favorite games, knights, involved riding imaginary horses, with the girls using the long, straight "ribs" of dead saguaro cacti as lances.

Another relaxing activity for Ned Danson was visiting shops, especially art galleries and Southwestern arts and crafts stores. Even if only window shopping, he loved perusing beautiful items and talking with the proprietors.

This activity proved useful when Danson assigned the students in his Museum Methods class the task of creating an exhibit called "Spanish Colonial Treasures" for the Arizona State Museum. Through his contacts with collectors, his own parish church, and Father Kino's 18th century San Xavier Mission south of Tucson, Danson and his students brought together fur-

Danson preparing for the Museum Methods Class "Spanish Colonial Treasures" exhibit at the Arizona State Museum, fall 1953

KEEP IN MIND, MY SON
For every PhD., there is an
equal and opposite PhD.

Card given to Ned Danson after receiving his doctorate; pictured is his mother, Ann Allen Danson, in her twenties

niture, paintings, religious art and other religious paraphernalia
from the Spanish Colonial era. Danson also borrowed pieces
from Clay Lockett, a collector of Southwestern and Spanish Colonial arts. Lockett had been a classmate of Emil Haury at the
University of Arizona and had gone on to operate an Indian
crafts store in Tucson in the winter and spend his summers in
Flagstaff. Danson spent so much time with another of the collectors, Jane Ivancovich, that Jan enjoyed marching around the
family home singing, "Daddy loves Jane Ivancovich."

The summer after receiving his Ph.D., Danson returned to Point
of Pines as a member of the staff. He spent the next four summers
at Point of Pines, becoming Assistant Director of the field school his
second year and running the school himself in 1954, while Haury
attended meetings in Europe. Besides helping Haury administer the
camp and the excavations, he taught some of the weekday classes,
held after dinner. Every two weeks, he would drive the hundred miles
across rough and sometimes muddy dirt roads to Globe, Arizona, to
buy food for the archaeology students and staff, pick up mail, and
visit the library to check out books for his children.

One of those trips proved more of an adventure than the
others. "I went to town [Globe] last Wednesday to shop and
pick up Molly Thompson," Danson wrote his family, "and on
returning on Thursday we hit a flash flood in Park Cabin Creek
18 miles from camp. After waiting 2 1/2 hours we drove ahead
through 2 crossings (there are 26 in all) only to get stuck in
the 3rd. . . . There we sat—I called on a power-line telephone
to Black River for help—the water was running through the
floor-boards of the car." While waiting for the rescue crew, they
were helped by a group of Apache cowboys who "lassoed our
bumper and pulled us out . . . " of the creek. But the car was
dead and night was falling. It took until 10:30 PM for the Black
River power truck to arrive. While waiting for them, Danson,
his pants soaked from wading in the creek, put on a fresh pair
of trousers, "preserving," as the Thompsons later put it, "his
reputation for sartorial elegance even on a pitch black night."

University of Arizona Archaeological Field School, Point of Pines, Arizona, 1952

Ted Danson's first role, playing the groom at Emil and Hulda Haury's 25th wedding anniversary, Point of Pines, 1953; Janet Burner as Hulda

In a letter to his mother, Danson wrote:

> We got home at one AM. . . . Fourteen hours to get
> home! Spent the entire next day with all the men re-
> building roads—which washed out the following night,
> but not until the Doctor left and some guests came in.
> Repaired the truck the next day. It took 5 men 6 hours
> to clean the mud out. I've never seen so much rain. All's
> well now & camp is back in order again & archaeology,
> not road and rescue work is getting done!

Because Ted had been considered too young to be at Point
of Pines in 1952, Jessica and the children went to see her family
in Laguna Beach, instead. But they spent the next three summers
at the field school. Jessica loved the pine trees that reminded her
of her summers spent by Puget Sound, enjoyed the students and
was grateful not to have to cook meals. A lover of wild nature,
Jessica was thrilled by the powerful summer thunderstorms that
swept across the prairie from the White Mountains. One day in
their cabin, she heard thunder crashing outside and threw open
the door, beckoned to her children and called out, 'Isn't this
glorious?" That was fine with Ned, but when she walked out to
stand under a lone pine tree on the edge of the prairie during an
intense lightning storm, he scolded her for setting a dangerous
example for the students.

These summers at Point of Pines also gave Jan Danson and
Dr. Haury's son Loren—her future husband—time to get to
know one another. But at the time, neither of the Danson children
attracted much of Loren's attention. In the hierarchy of Point
of Pines children he was a "frog." They were considered "tad-
poles" or "tads."

Yet, despite that division, Jan and Ted, and all the other
children in camp, did their part. While Loren was digging with
the students, the young children were assigned to pick up chewing gum wrappers and cigarette butts. And Jan and Ted made a

Point of Pines staff and crew, 1954

Top Row (left to right): Dan Sheans, Galen Baker, Phil Olsen, Dr Martin Withers, Linda McIlvain, Jalil Jawad, Paul Buss

2nd Row: Herbert Lewis, Bob Wallace, Wes Ferguson, Bill Beeson, Frank Holzcamper, Tacoma Sloan, Virginia Clyde, Ray Thompson

3rd Row: Jim, Jimmie and Jessie Williams, Pat Dunbar, Star Miller, Mrs. Withers, Jessica and Ned Danson, Loren Haury, Dave and Barbara Breternitz

On Ground: Jimmie Withers, Ted Danson, Ann and Sally Withers, Jan Danson

game of searching the ground at the nearby site for arrowheads
or beads lying on the surface. As camp policy dictated, they
showed everything they found to Dr. Haury, who confiscated
all the interesting pieces for study. And, although they did not
receive the full education in archaeology given to the students,
they learned much and participated in camp life. Jan enjoyed attending the archaeology lectures in the evenings and joined the
students at the Saturday night square dances. Young Ted Danson acted for the first time at the field school, portraying Emil
Haury during a reenacted wedding to celebrate Emil and Hulda
Haury's 25th anniversary. He later performed in a play about an
Incan prince, which had been written by his sister.

In 1953, after Point of Pines, Ned Danson returned to
teaching in Tucson. That same year, he was elected to the Museum of Northern Arizona's Board of Trustees. "I think that I
was asked to be on the board, one, because Emil [who was also
on the board] recommended me," Danson wrote, "two, Ferrell
Colton and I had a common interest in sailing, three, they wanted some 'younger' blood on the board, and four, the Coltons
knew us. . . ."

The Museum of Northern Arizona had been founded in
1928, when a group of leading Flagstaff citizens, including the
Coltons, decided to provide an institution of learning for the
small but growing community. Concerned that Northern Arizona's archaeological treasures were being plundered for collections around the world, they established "The Northern Arizona Society of Science and Art." The Society's goals, as stated
in its constitution, were "to maintain in the City of Flagstaff a
museum, to protect historic and prehistoric sites, works of art,
scenic places, and wildlife . . . and to provide facilities for research and publication."

After Dr. Colton was selected by the group to be the first
director, he and his wife, Mary-Russell, took the lead in shaping
the institution into, in Danson's words, an "institution to which
scientists, writers and artists, professors and students, could

Dr Harold Colton breaking ground for a new building at the Museum of Northern Arizona's Research Center, 1953. (Left to right) Unknown, Carlie Mallet, Dorothy Pollock, Robert Euler, Ned Danson, Mrs Colton, Agnes Allen, and Dr Colton

Jesssica and Ned in front of the fireplace in their Tucson home, 1956

come to do research, study and learn about one of the most fascinating areas in the world."

That area was the Colorado Plateau, a geographical area encompassing most of northern Arizona, southeastern Utah, and parts of Colorado and New Mexico. The Plateau provided ample opportunity for research in a variety of disciplines. Sitting on its southern edge, Flagstaff was, as Danson described it:

> Within 30 miles of . . . land [that] rose from 4,000 feet to over 12,000. . . . The Mountain was a cloud-producer, and studies of meteorology were done at the Museum for many years. With the Grand Canyon nearby, the geologic layers of the earth were laid out like a sandwich for scientists to explore. Early dinosaurs are found nearby and early life forms can be examined in the exposed walls of the Grand Canyon. Add to that the native cultures that lived nearby and you had a perfect place to study the earth, the plants and animals that lived on the earth, the climate, and man.

The original Museum of Northern Arizona was small, occupying two rooms in the Flagstaff Woman's Club. After six years, Mrs. Colton donated some of the farmland she owned north of Flagstaff for a new museum building, designed by Dr. Colton in a Spanish Colonial/Pueblo Revival style. The new Museum of Northern Arizona opened in 1936. At the entrance to the building, they placed a sign: "We display ideas, not things." For many years, the Society's research facilities were divided between the Museum building and Dr. Colton's private office next to his home.

But the Museum as an institution focused on more than science. Due in large part to the influence of Mary-Russell Ferrell Colton, already a prominent painter, the Museum was equally dedicated to studying and promoting the art of all the peoples of the Colorado Plateau, from Native Americans past and present, to visiting artists who came from all over the world for inspiration.

When Ned Danson joined the Museum's board, the staff was small, with fewer than ten employees, including those who worked there only in the summer. Weekly staff meetings were held around the Coltons' dining room table. With such a small staff, Harold Colton was more the head of a scientific family than a traditional administrator of an institution. Formal rules and structures were few. Researchers were free to pursue whatever interested them, even if they were not formally trained in the discipline. Dr. Colton, a retired professor of zoology, became an expert on archaeology, Hopi katsina dolls, and other aspects of ethnology. The long-time paleontology curator, Lionel "Major" Brady had studied basic geology at Cambridge and then served many years as headmaster of a boy's school.

But by the early 1950s, the United States in general and the American West in particular had started to reshape themselves culturally and physically. This new West affected the Museum. New highways, pipelines and power lines were being built on Federal land throughout the West, which, by law, required salvage archaeology—the recovery of artifacts and information from construction rights-of-way—be done before sites were destroyed to make way for new projects. At the same time, a surge in the number of people studying science was bringing more researchers to the Museum to use its facilities and to request space to store their specimens.

In his annual report to the Board of Trustees, Colton wrote about the Museum's gradual growth.

> 1952 has been a year of decision for the Museum. . . .
> We have proceeded slowly until this small institution
> has assumed responsibilities that have consumed all the
> time of its small staff, making it impossible for them to
> contribute individually to our knowledge by scientific
> research for which they were trained. All they did was
> to administer the research of others.

By the time Ned Danson joined the Museum's board in 1953, it was formulating a vision of how the Museum could grow while supervising the ever increasing number of researchers. That year, ground was broken on a new building across the road from the Museum on land Mrs. Colton had donated after the war. The land had already been used to house visiting scientists and students. But, with completion of the new building in 1954, with space for laboratories, collections, a library and administrative offices, the Museum's Research Center, as it was called, came into its own. While the Museum still functioned as a community, it was starting to take on the forms of a traditional, if still small, institution. As Dr. Colton put it, the Museum of Northern Arizona was now physically "organized into two parts with separate functions, a museum of science and art . . . and a research center devoted to increasing our knowledge of the natural resources of northern Arizona." In 1954, Colton said, "For 25 years the Museum had been like a caterpillar, eating and growing. [This year] the Museum resembled a chrysalis, in a cocoon, reorganizing its structure in preparation of the butterfly to come."

But even though Colton could see how the Museum ought to change, that did not mean he felt he was the one to bring that change about. His health was starting to decline, as was his wife's. He could no longer devote the energy that he once had to running an expanding Museum while pursuing his own research.

Additionally, as Ned Danson later put it, although Dr. Colton loved to pursue science and had proved an excellent father to a small scientific family, he had no interest in being a traditional administrator of a formally structured institution. And this was what the Museum was becoming.

In 1956, three years after Danson joined the Museum's Board of Trustees, the assistant director announced he would resign to begin work on his Ph.D. With Colton openly speaking of retirement, the board decided that the Museum should hire a new assistant director who would spend several years under Dr. Colton's guidance, eventually taking over as director when Colton decided to retire.

Following the board meeting where this was discussed, Danson drove Emil Haury—also a board member—and both of their wives back to Tucson. During the trip, Jessica asked Haury who he thought should be Dr. Colton's successor.

Haury pointed straight at Ned.

For years, Jessica, who had loved living in Tucson, considered asking that question to be one of her worst mistakes. Ned, by contrast, was convinced by the end of the car trip.

Haury had had time to hone his arguments. He and Colton had been writing to each other about the matter of the Museum's succession since the previous year. In a letter, Haury suggested Danson to Colton, who replied, "When we were looking for some one to ultimately take over the directorship here, when I step down, we immediately thought of Ned but on account of your breaking him in as your second in command we decided not to approach him. . . . Mary-Russell and I are therefore most happy to receive your suggestion. . . ."

Ned Danson was formally invited to become assistant director in February, 1956. "I was enthusiastic about the opportunity," he wrote later. But in accepting the job, he would be making many sacrifices for himself and his family. They would have to leave the beautiful Tucson home that they loved. The new job would come at a lower salary. And it was not a teaching position. As Danson was finalizing his plans, Watson Smith, now living in Tucson, came to speak to him. Commenting that he considered Danson to be a superb teacher, Smith warned him that, if he took this new position, he would be giving up being a professor forever. Danson acknowledged the warning but accepted the job.

Entrance to the Museum of Northern Arizona

CHAPTER THREE

IDEAS, NOT THINGS

Assistant Director of the Museum of Northern Arizona
1956 - 1958

Ned Danson left his position at the University of Arizona to become the Museum of Northern Arizona's new assistant director at the end of the spring semester. He and his family, including their dog Patches, moved from Tucson to Flagstaff on June 1, 1956, and took up residence in the Museum's two-story homestead directly across the road from the Museum.

The Homestead—short for the Thomas F. McMillan Homestead after its first owner—was a hand-adzed log house and one of the oldest pioneer era buildings in Flagstaff. In 1886, McMillan had built a two-story log cabin out of ponderosa pine cut on his property. But when his wife arrived from Tennessee, she refused to live in a "log cabin." So her husband covered the sides with clapboard and added a lean-to on the back and covered porches on the front. In 1927, when the Coltons purchased the Homestead, the building was dilapidated. Some of the rooms had recently been used to house chickens. The Coltons had the Homestead renovated and deeded it to the Museum.

The Homestead's age and historical significance delighted Jessica. She would later note how old it was when her mother-in-law was visiting, only to hear Ann Danson ask her not to say that, as she was six years older than the building.

Before the Dansons arrived, the Homestead had again been renovated. A new furnace was installed and wallboards removed

The Thomas F. McMillan Homestead, Flagstaff, Arizona

Homestead den, early 1970s

Homestead living room, early 1970s

from the thick log walls in the downstairs den. Despite the work the Coltons had put into the house, its floorboards still creaked and the floors lacked insulation. The Dansons endured many cold winters with chilly rooms and frozen pipes. And as Ted grew, the low, sharply sloping ceiling of his upstairs bedroom became more and more of a problem for him.

Ned Danson's first month in Flagstaff was busy. Apart from the usual tasks required by a move, he spent the month meeting the people at the Museum and its Research Center. Some of the staff were familiar to Danson. The curator of anthropology, David Breternitz, had been Danson's student in Tucson and Jan and Ted's occasional babysitter. Katharine Bartlett, the Museum's librarian and part of the small support staff, had been with the Museum since 1930, serving as Dr. Colton's assistant in archaeology. And Milton Wetherill, one of the custodians and the technician who collected and catalogued the animals, insects and reptiles for the Museum's collections, was a member of a family of cowboy-explorers and guides to archeologists known throughout the Southwest.

"It was a small but dedicated staff," Danson later wrote, "and I enjoyed working with them all." To oversee the Museum's operations, Danson set up his office in a big room at the rear of the Museum building, near that of Barton Wright, the Museum's curator, a former student of anthropology at the University of Arizona who had drawn some of the maps and illustrations for Danson's dissertation. "Barton," Danson wrote later, "was truly brilliant and his exhibitions were of high quality, especially his science exhibitions that came at the end of each year."

Summer was the busiest season for the Museum, a time when independent researchers and visiting college students lived on Museum property for the summer and other scientists came for shorter periods. Among the growing number of independent researchers, graduate students and summer assistants that first summer were people who would return to the Museum later during Danson's tenure, including University of

Arizona geology student William "Bill" Breed, and Hermann Bleibtreu, a Harvard student helping dig an archaeological site on a nearby ranch.

That summer, the Dansons entertained numerous guests, most for meals, many for the night. On their second night in the Homestead, Danson brought a visiting anthropologist home for dinner and to spend the night in the den.

A number of the guests were speakers from the "Tuesday seminars," held during the summers at the Research Center. Dr. Colton arranged for a different member of the Museum staff or a visiting expert to give a talk each week. That first summer, Ned Danson began his tradition of inviting the speaker to the Homestead for drinks and sometimes a candlelight dinner. Jessica would usually serve roast beef, and Ned would tell stories about his adventures on the schooner *Yankee* or about his family in Cincinnati, casually announcing, "My father was a bachelor," pausing to let the words sink in as he sharpened the carving knife on his father's steel before weaving the rest of his story and serving the roast.

Over the course of almost two decades at the Museum, the Dansons had guests nearly twice a week. And Ned Danson took pride in making the Homestead a beautiful place to visit. "Little by little we fixed up the yard," he wrote, "planted a rock garden and a lawn, put up fences, and made it possible to entertain large groups out of doors. Smaller groups were entertained in the living room and den and, if they were staying for dinner, the dining room. With soft off-white walls, tan draperies and [a] carpet of heavy geometric patterns, and our paintings and books, the house took on a cozy look."

Danson's second month started with his first Hopi Show. Held each year over the Fourth of July weekend, the show started on the night before the public opening with the staff assembling in the Museum's lobby to greet Museum members for the preview night. "When the doors finally opened, members flooded into the Museum," Danson's daughter recalled. "They

Ned Danson (left) and Mrs. Colton (center) judging crafts before the 1959 Hopi Craftsman Show

Ned visiting a trading post on the Navajo Reservation

were greeted by Dr. and Mrs. Danson and other staff members and then rushed off to see the show. Most of the best works were purchased that night."

In the patio, Barton Wright arranged blankets, pottery, weavings and other works of art, according to the village the artists came from, allowing visitors to understand the stylistic variations between the different Hopi Mesas. To learn more, visitors were also able to speak with Museum scientists and to the Hopi exhibiters themselves.

The Coltons had started the Hopi Show (officially the "Hopi Craftsman Exhibition") in 1930 to promote and stimulate a market for Hopi arts and crafts in response to a concern that the skills to make them could become lost. With the growing availability of store-bought household goods, there was less need to learn how to make traditional utilitarian or finely decorated pottery or baskets using traditional vegetable dyes. The Coltons, working with the Hopi, helped to turn this around. Museum staff traveled regularly to the reservations to encourage craftsmen to send their best works to sell at the shows.

Sometimes they did more than provide a market. Dr. Colton studied pottery firing techniques and shared his findings with the Hopi. Mrs. Colton not only researched Hopi dyes, but collaborated with the Museum's Curator of Art, Virgil Hubert, and Hopi silversmiths, in the development of a new style of silver work—Hopi overlay. Less reminiscent of Navajo silver, and drawing instead on traditional Hopi pottery designs, the new silver was more culturally specific to Hopi and of greater interest to customers.

Years later, Danson wrote about his first Hopi Show:

Barton Wright, aided by his wife Margaret, and Katharine Bartlett, were on duty throughout the show. Jessica was there as a relief and so was I. Other staff members, summer assistants, and [a] few old friends helped with the selling and talking to the crowds who wanted to know more about the crafts and the craftsmen. In the patio, a weaver, a potter, and several basket makers, all in traditional Hopi clothing, demonstrated their crafts.

This was a wonderful exhibition, and the patio of the Museum was a beautiful place to have it. Silver making and kachina doll [now called katsina doll] carving was done in the Special Exhibit room. The weaving, baskets and kachinas had to be protected from the rain squalls which invariably came during the exhibitions, when there would be a rush to lower the canvas that edged the patio.

Hopi Shows always drew large crowds, even though, at the time, regular Museum attendance was not as large as it would later become when highway construction made the road past the Museum one of the routes to the Grand Canyon. This was not only due to the interest in the arts and crafts the Museum had helped foster, but also because the show coincided with the All-Indian Pow-Wow held in Flagstaff over the Fourth of July holiday.

The day after Danson's first Hopi Show opened, Dr. Colton called Ned to his office to tell him he was about to have cancer surgery. "One month on the job," Danson recalled, "and I was in charge. It was a tremendous challenge, and it was typical of Dr. Colton's thoughtfulness to put off telling me until the show was going." Fortunately, Colton recuperated quickly and was ready in mid-August to welcome attendees to the Pecos Conference, the yearly gathering of Southwestern field archaeologists, hosted that year by the Museum.

"That was the beginning of a busy summer, a busy year, and a busy life," Danson recalled, adding, "And a wonderful one it was."

And the shows for the year were not over. A few weeks later in July, the Museum held its Navajo Craftsman Exhibition. Though not coinciding with a Pow-Wow and, therefore, smaller, the Navajo Show lasted a full week instead of a few days. It provided a chance for outsiders to come to understand the Navajo people, their art and their culture. And it stimulated a market for Navajo pottery and basketry, while increasing sales for jewelry and handwoven wool rugs, two Navajo crafts that already were widely appreciated.

"These exhibitions," Danson wrote, "became famous and have been copied throughout the West. I well remember being asked by the Heard Museum if MNA would mind if another institution held a similar exhibition at a different time of the year."

The shows, particularly the Hopi Show, forged bonds between the tribes and the Museum, bonds that Danson and his family quickly grew to share. Several Hopi craftsmen worked as support staff at the Museum, living on the Museum and Research Center grounds with their families. Danson became close to katsina doll carver, drummer and Museum custodian "Jimmy K" Kewanwytewa, as well as his colleague Willie Coin, a Hopi silversmith and weaver. But relationships with staff and Native peoples were only part of an assistant director's duties. Danson also forged relationships with other residents of the community.

In his first month at the Museum, at Colton's invitation, Danson started regularly attending the weekly Flagstaff Rotary Club meetings. As in all social situations, he thrived, finding both useful business contacts and enjoying getting to know new people. Danson became active in the Flagstaff community in other ways. In his second year, he began a decades-long membership on the board of the Flagstaff Symphony, and that same year he was elected to the local Episcopal Church's vestry, where he served for twelve years.

As assistant director and later director, Danson kept in close communication with Dr. Colton. They began a tradition of weekly Tuesday morning meetings in Colton's office next door to the director's home. "It was a wonderful book lined room," Danson later wrote. "It had paintings above the books on one wall and over the fireplace, and there was a large picture window looking out at the San Francisco Peaks." About Colton, Danson said, "Doctor Colton was a gentle, intelligent man with great curiosity and a love of knowledge. He had a delightful sense of humor—quiet but always there."

On Danson's arrival, Colton began relinquishing some of his duties. Danson took on his administrative responsibilities, and the Board hired an editor for the Museum's magazine, *Plateau*, as well as for its technical publications.

One of the many tasks Danson inherited from Colton was overseeing salvage archaeology in Northern Arizona. For years, Arizona law had given authority for salvage archaeology oversight to the Arizona State Museum at the University of Arizona. But after World War II, salvage archaeology increased to the point that the University could not handle the work on its own. Dr. Haury made an arrangement with Dr. Colton to divide supervision of salvage archeology in the state between the University and the Museum. Creation in 1956 of the interstate highway program, as well as plans for additional gas pipelines and changes in railroad rights-of-way, further added to the archaeologists' workload.

Even though both federal and state law mandated that salvage archaeology be done, Danson realized that this did not mean it always took place. As roads were built, he discovered that project engineers often failed to notify scientists about the existence of archaeological sites until they dug up something of obvious importance. Therefore, Danson occasionally drove one of his cars—he had two at the time, an International Harvester Travelall and a Pontiac woodie station wagon—to check up on the construction crews. He crossed Northern Arizona, visiting construction sites and rights-of-way, writing down the infractions he found and reporting them to the Arizona State Museum.

One of the largest salvage archaeology projects the Museum became involved with during Danson's years began in 1956, when a National Park Service archaeologist "came over from Santa Fe to talk about the chances of the Museum taking over the archaeological and geological work in Glen Canyon. The Bureau of Reclamation had finally received the funding to build a large dam on the Colorado River." The dam would inundate Glen Canyon, a pristine wilderness of river-carved sandstone with large prehistoric sites and petroglyph-covered cliffs. The next year the Museum began work on the Glen Canyon Project for the National Park Service.

Under archaeologist William "Bill" Adams, and later, Alexander "Lex" Lindsay, another of Danson's former University of Arizona graduate students, the Museum surveyed and excavated sites along the south side of the Colorado River, while the University of Utah was responsible for the north side. In order to understand the cultural history of the area, the Museum also surveyed and excavated prehistoric dwellings on the mesas above the Canyon. After seven years, the diversion tunnel was closed, and Lake Powell began to flood the canyon. The active phase of the Glen Canyon Project was over, except for the completion of reports describing what was being lost under the lake and integrating the cultural material they had salvaged into the Museum's collection.

Another major program that began in Danson's first year at the Museum grew out of a conversation with two visiting Indiana University linguists, Drs. Carl and Florence Voegelin. "Thanks to a long talk with Carl and Florence. . . ," Danson wrote, "the idea of having co-operating agreements with universities was born. Students could be given credit by their university for their work at the Museum during the summer. It grew to be an important part of the Museum's summer program." By 1972, fourteen such agreements with schools such as the University of Colorado, Indiana University, the University of Illinois and Colombia University had been signed. This program helped increase the number and diversity of people making use of the Museum's Research Center.

One scientist working at the Research Center during Danson's early years at the Museum was British geologist Dr. Keith

Runcorn. Runcorn sometimes worked alone and, at other times, was assisted by graduate students like Bruce Babbitt, a member of a Flagstaff ranching family close to the Museum. Babbitt later went on to become Governor of Arizona and also United States Secretary of the Interior. "Runcorn," Danson wrote, "would collect examples of basalt from recent [a millennium old] lava flows at Sunset Crater [a dormant cinder cone near Flagstaff] to the oldest deposits he could find. Before he removed a piece, he would measure the magnetic north and mark it on the specimen. . . ." The body of evidence Runcorn was amassing would eventually help revolutionize geology.

With the coming of spring, the Museum began to prepare actively for its yearly shows. The first was the Junior Indian Art Show. One of the earliest shows of its kind, it had been created by Mrs. Colton to promote art by Native Americans from age six to eighteen. Displaying art made in schools both on and off the reservations, the Museum not only offered prizes but also purchased some of the works for the collection. Danson continued this tradition for the duration of his time at the Museum.

But the Museum's two big events remained the Hopi and Navajo shows. And in 1957, for the first time, Ned Danson was fully involved in the preparations for those events. Dr. and Mrs. Colton had started the tradition of visiting Hopi artists in their home villages in May, reminding them of the upcoming show and then returning in June to select the best pieces. The new assistant director took up that tradition, accompanying Barton Wright and other staff members to the mesas. It was an experience he fondly remembered later in life:

> We usually started collecting at Moencopi. It wouldn't take long before the whole village would know we were out. Jimmy Kewanwytewa was our usual [guide]. Those days on the reservation with him were wondrous experiences. It was always exciting to get the pottery being made at First Mesa [the easternmost of the three mesas

with Hopi villages on them]. Rena Kavena, Patty Maho, Garnet Pavatea and others would have things put away for us: bowls and jars of all sizes. I was always amazed at the amount of lovely perfect pieces of pottery that we could collect.

Over time, Ned Danson developed a network of friendships and partnerships with the Hopi. In addition to collecting the best works for the Hopi Show, he bought for himself pieces of pottery that he liked, despite their being cracked or smudged during firing. And Danson received warm hospitality in the villages, being welcomed into Hopi homes and generously being given gifts. He evoked peals of laughter when his attempts to speak a few words of Hopi went wrong. He sometimes even used words and phrases that were to be spoken only by women.

Collecting trips for the Navajo Show were different. The Navajo lived in remote family compounds, spread across their vast reservation, making it impractical to visit individual craftsmen. Instead, Museum staff visited trading posts across the Reservation to find good examples of rugs, baskets, jewelry and other Navajo crafts. After the show was over, staff returned unsold items to the trading posts. Danson enjoyed personally returning the items to those posts closest to Flagstaff. He loved talking to the traders, examining their rugs and jewelry, and, whenever possible, looking in the pawn rooms where he could see some of the oldest and best jewelry.

Despite the immense effort he and the rest of the Museum staff put in at that time of the year, Danson took moments to appreciate the beauty in which he found himself. In a letter he wrote to his mother, while waiting for Museum visitors to arrive for one of his first Navajo shows, he told her, "The cumulous clouds are beginning to pile up over the San Francisco Peaks and another lovely Arizona day is really getting under way. I do love this country and its beauty and I never get tired of the life here." He confessed to her that, "I only wish some times that I had more time just to sit and do nothing and enjoy it. Essentially I'm lazy and would much rather be a good-for-nothing, but unfortunately, you endowed me with a sense of responsibility and I just don't feel right doing nothing for long."

After the two craftsmen shows ended and summer research wound down, life at the Museum became quieter. In those years, the Museum was closed for two months in the winter, which gave Barton Wright time to refurbish displays and prepare for coming special exhibits. Ned and Jessica began a tradition of hosting a Christmas party for staff in mid-December. Before Christmas, the Dansons, sometimes accompanied by staff, cut down their own Christmas tree in the nearby Coconino National Forest. Christmas itself remained a family affair, with the usual Danson abundance of presents and overstuffed stockings, and attendance at the Christmas church service.

Particularly energized by the cold weather was the dog Patches. After years in the Tucson heat, the weary, old dog regained the energy of a puppy and raced around the snowy ground. She had company now, as the Danson family had inherited a second dog with the Homestead—a mutt named Piki, after the thin cornmeal bread Hopis traditionally baked on a heated rock.

After a year at the Homestead, Patches died, leaving Piki as the family's only dog. Jan recalled that "Piki was an independent dog, but frightened by Flagstaff's frequent summer lightning storms. As soon as he heard thunder, he would dive under the closest bed."

The remainder of the Danson household adapted more readily to Flagstaff and the Museum. Ted quickly became close friends with Willie Coin's son, Raymond. Ted's other close friends included Marc Gaede, a young relative of a Museum archaeologist and a future staff photographer, and other Museum children. As well as entertaining guests, Jessica cleaned the cabins each spring to prepare for summer assistants and research fellows, and provided food and lodging for sick staff members. One day, Jan came home from school to find the wife of a Muse-

Jessica and Piki in Homestead garden

Ted on horseback in front of the Homestead, 1957

Ted and friends in Homestead dining room. (Left to right) Raymond Coin, Jack Metzger, Jan, Marc Gaede and Ted, about 1960

um archaeologist on the sofa bed in the living room being nursed by Jessica as she recovered from oral surgery. And when Jessica learned that two of the students working at the Museum for the summer were in love, she invited them over to the Homestead to baby-sit long after her children were old enough for it not to be necessary. Just so the two could be together.

Years later, the two students, now married, wrote, "Jessica Danson was an essential presence, providing a depth and beauty of character and spirit that nourished Ned, their children, and their friends."

Jan spent much of her time in the summers attending the Tuesday Seminars by Research Center scientists. She also volunteered at the Museum before the Hopi and Navajo Shows, assisting Barton Wright, Mrs. Colton, Clay Lockett and others in laying out crafts for judging and then working in sales during the exhibitions. She also attended Hopi dances in July, usually with members of the staff, rather than her parents, because summers were often too busy for Ned and Jessica to get away from the Museum.

During the family's second summer in Flagstaff, Danson borrowed two horses from his uncle at Kenyon Ranch. Jan rode occasionally, but Ted and Raymond spent the summer exploring the Research Center and nearby Coyote Range on horseback. Keeping the horses proved to be problematic. The animals discovered weaknesses in the split rail fences enclosing the Homestead's field. Many mornings, the horses were found loose on the road separating the Homestead from the Museum. Whenever this happened, Ned and Ted had to chase them down, herding them off the road before they were struck by the huge logging trucks speeding past the Museum. Ted recalled that, on those mornings, his father mostly acted in a supervisory capacity.

The Danson family also made personal friends in Flagstaff. They frequently socialized with the Episcopal Church's rectors. Herman Hurley, the Navajo foster son of one of the rectors, became Ted's good friend and skiing buddy. Dorothy Pollock, head of a prominent Flagstaff ranching family and a long-time member of the Museum's Board of Trustees, had children the same age as the Dansons'. Often staying in the Homestead when they were in town from their ranch, her family and the Dansons became close. Through church, Ned Danson came to know another ranching family, the Metzgers. After the two families became friends, Jane Metzger, the family matriarch, volunteered at the Research Center, and was elected to the Museum's Board of Trustees. Her son Jack, who would later become a Museum board member, joined Ted's circle of close friends.

The Dansons and Metzgers developed a Christmas-night tradition of sharing a turkey sandwich known to Ned Danson as a "Withy," named after the Glendale Withenbury family that E. B. and Ann Allen Danson had spent their Christmases with when Ned was still known as "Boy" Danson.

When the Metzgers visited the Homestead, the two families often played Charades. It was a game the Dansons played with many of their guests. The children loved it when one of the family chose *Andivius Hedulio*, the title of the obscure book about the Roman nobleman, that their father had read to them years earlier. When playing with the uninitiated, this virtually ensured that only members of the Danson family would be able to guess the title.

A less conventional game the family enjoyed playing with their friends and Museum staff carried the ominous name of "Murder." Played in the Homestead at night, with the lights off and the floorboards creaking with every step, the house could become, as Danson put it, "a very spooky, black and mysterious place." The family put that effect to good use.

The rules were simple. Players drew cards to determine who would be the designated murderer and who would be the district attorney. While the murderer's identity remained concealed, the district attorney went upstairs to the master bedroom and closed the door. Downstairs lights were turned off, and everyone else wandered around in the dark until the murderer mock-killed the victim, who screamed. Then everyone froze in place—only the murderer being allowed to move around to choose a deceptive freezing point. The district attorney came down the stairs and turned on the lights, then, in order to identify the murderer, went around questioning people about what they saw and heard. The victim could say nothing. Only the murderer was allowed to lie.

There were many memorable games of Murder. In one, murderer Ted, not having reached his full height, climbed up on a stool in order to reach his victim. As his hands closed around his victim's neck, the man started walking away, pulling Ted off the stool. Ted ended up squeezing the man's neck too realistically. When the lights were turned on, the victim was on his knees, gasping for air. Another time, Ned's nephew, Dan Perin, was the murderer. He decided to go after his Uncle Ned. He came upon his uncle in the dark and convinced him that he wasn't the murderer, then suggested they hide together in the Homestead's tiny, downstairs bathroom. Only then did Perin strike. Upon being strangled, Danson fell on his nephew, pinning him to the ground for an easy investigation by the district attorney.

Entertaining groups, large or small, was a prospect that energized Ned Danson, who loved playing host and charming people. However, the same atmosphere that energized the host drained the hostess. Jessica had always loved solitude, but felt bound to provide hospitality—both by a sense of duty and her own inborn desire to give of herself. Her respites from the efforts were few, primarily involving the yearly summer trips she and the children made to the California coast to visit her parents and her sister Eileen's family.

The family's morning routine at the Homestead was similar to that in Tucson. The children still joined their parents in bed after they had all awakened. Instead of coffee, however, Jessica and Ned, as children of British fathers, now often shared a pot of tea as they discussed the coming day with Jan and Ted. The morning rush often required the entire family to be in the bathroom getting ready at once. When Danson shaved and then dressed in his suit and tie, if he were in an especially good mood, he sang "Oh what a beautiful mornin', Oh what a beautiful day, I got a wonderful feelin', Ev'rything's goin' my way," a song he had fallen in love with upon seeing *Oklahoma!* while visiting New York during his days at Harvard.

After leaving the Homestead and driving to his office, originally in the Museum building and later at the Research Center, Danson assumed the responsibilities that Colton had found so draining, administering the growing research projects in an increasing number of disciplines.

The proximity of the Homestead to the Museum and Research Center buildings occasionally added to Danson's workload. He was sometimes called to fulfill mundane tasks, such as providing toilet paper rolls to the bathrooms in the Research Center. And his own sense of duty compelled him to lock the gate to the Museum property at night if he saw that the staff had forgotten to do so at the end of the day.

Another responsibility sent Danson driving across Arizona and beyond—the need to add to the Museum's collections. The boom in Indian arts that the Coltons helped foster led to collectors amassing large, private collections. One of the larger ones in the 1950s belonged to Mr. and Mrs. Harold Gladwin. Gladwin had been a Wall Street investor who got out before the great crash of 1929 and moved west. Gladwin became a friend of archaeologist Alfred V. Kidder and, by watching him work, developed a passion for the subject. With Kidder's counsel, Gladwin established the Gila Pueblo Archaeological Foundation in Globe, Arizona, where he sponsored archaeological research and amassed substantial collections of archaeological and contemporary Indian arts and crafts. The latter included Navajo rugs and silver, Pueblo pottery, and other types of Indian art. Many museums in the Southwest coveted the collection. Soon after joining the Museum, Danson had begun corresponding with Mrs. Gladwin and had later traveled to the Gladwin home in Santa Barbara, California, in hopes of securing their collections for the Museum.

But, not all of Danson's business trips were for the Museum. In 1958, he began serving on two boards that would play an important role in his life. The first was the Southwest Monuments Association—later renamed the Southwest Parks and Monuments Association—which promoted research and published books and pamphlets for the smaller national parks and monuments in the Southwest. Senator Barry Goldwater recommended Danson for the archaeologist's seat on the U.S. Department of Interior's Advisory Board on National Parks, Historic Sites, Buildings, and Monuments (informally, at the time, called the "National Park Service Advisory Board" and now known as the "National Park System Advisory Board"), a seat previously held by Ned's Harvard mentor, Jo Brew. The Board was created by Congress in 1939 to "recommend policies . . . pertaining to national parks and to the restoration, reconstruction, conservation and general administration of historic and archaeological buildings and properties."

Danson's membership on both of those boards would prove useful after he and Colton made a trip to Hubbell Trading Post, where Danson had stayed with his parents during his first trip to the West as a child. The Hubbell family, owners of the trading post, founded in 1876 by Don Lorenzo Hubbell, had entertained many famous artists over the years. "The post," Danson wrote to his mother, "is full of fabulously interesting historical, ethnographical and art objects. Every artist who painted in the Southwest around the end of the 19th century left a painting as a thank you for old Don Lorenzo's kindness and generosity." As a result, the Hubbell family had gathered a large personal collection of paintings.

Danson and Colton went there to meet with Ramon Hubbell, son of the original trader, to see if they could arrange a loan of some of the two-hundred red crayon sketches of Navajos and other Native Americans by artist E. A. Burbank. While Hubbell Trading Post had been a vibrant part of the Navajo Reservation economy for years, by 1957, it had fallen upon hard times. Ramon Hubbell, who had suffered a serious stroke, and his wife, Dorothy, no longer felt capable of running it.

At the end of their conversation, the Hubbells brought up the possibility of the Museum purchasing the trading post and their nearby home to preserve the property. Colton explained that the Museum was a private, scientific institution, and that such an acquisition was far beyond the Museum's means.

But when one path was closed, Danson found another. On their drive back to Flagstaff, he suggested to Colton that the trading post might prove a fine candidate to become a national monument. Then Danson did what he did so well: make connections. He wrote to the National Park Service with his idea and contacted Arizona's Congressional delegation, winning such diverse allies as Representative Stewart Udall and Arizona's two very different Senators—Democrat Carl Hayden and conservative icon Barry Goldwater. The two Senators disagreed on much, but Danson found they agreed on Hubbell. Udall, Goldwater and Danson established a close working relationship. And all three members of Congress, who had visited the trading post as youths, agreed that Hubbell Trading Post represented a critical point in the history of Arizona and the Navajo people, and that it must be preserved. In a letter to Danson, Goldwater said he considered it "superior to any other Post we ever visited," and, "in my mind that was just the way a Navajo post should look."

Two years later, the National Park Service Advisory Board, with Danson now a member, voted to recommend that Hubbell Trading Post become a National Historic Site, and a month later Senator Carl Hayden and Congressman Steward Udall introduced legislation in Congress. But the House bill was blocked for the next seven years by complaints from two congressmen from other states that a trading post on the Navajo Reservation was not historic and that the bill was "pork," not worth what the Hubbells were asking. One of the congressmen had unknowingly purchased fraudulent Indian arts from a different source and did not trust that the Hubbells' collection was worth

Rug Room, Hubbell Trading Post, Ganado, Arizona

Ned Danson and Dorothy Hubbell in Hubbell Trading Post

any more than his fakes. But, with allies in Congress and a seat at the table in the National Park Service, Danson continued to press his case.

To counter the argument that the Hubbell collection was not worth the price, Danson arranged in 1960, with Indian art experts and art gallery owners whose stores he had visited for years, to inventory and appraise the Hubbell's home. "The walls," of the house, he later wrote, "were covered with paintings by many of the well known artists of the day. There were lovely old Navajo rugs—some very large—on the floors, and some Hopi and Navajo baskets on the ceiling. The place was a veritable treasure house of Indian arts and crafts of the turn of the 19th century through the 1940s."

That year, Danson felt that Hubbell had a good chance of being accepted. But another site in Arizona, Fort Bowie, was also being considered for incorporation into the national park system. The risk of neither one being accepted, if Arizona's national parks' advocates divided their efforts, was high. So despite his work promoting the Hubbell purchase, Danson decided that the fort was the better candidate at the time. He wrote to Goldwater, saying that he would temporarily cease his advocacy for Hubbell until the Fort Bowie bill passed.

With Fort Bowie declared a National Historic Landmark in late 1960, Danson resumed his advocacy for Hubbell. Legislation to purchase the trading post failed in both 1961 and 1962.

In 1965, with Stewart Udall now Secretary of the Interior and Danson believing the time was finally right, bills to purchase the trading post were introduced again, and Danson went to Congress to testify before Congressional committees. By this time, he did not want Hubbell to become a static museum. He envisioned it continuing as a working trading post while under government protection.

Congress passed and President Johnson signed the bill that year, making the Hubbell Trading Post a National Historic Site. Congressman Morris Udall, now holding his brother Stewart

Udall's House seat, sent Ned Danson a pen the President had used to sign the bill, writing, "This is something you deserve."

Even after the bill was passed, there were problems. The National Park Service did not want to be responsible for operating a "living trading post." And it was having difficulty finding an organization that would fulfill that function for them on a long-term basis. Finally, a National Park Service representative called "his old friend, Dr. Edward B. Danson...." According to the National Park Service's administrative history of the Hubbell Trading Post, "The ubiquitous Ned Danson was not only Director of the Museum of Northern Arizona and a member of the National Parks Advisory Board, he was also on the Board of Directors of Southwest Parks and Monuments Association [SPMA]!" They asked him if SPMA would be able to run the trading post. Although this was not the original purpose of SPMA, Danson and the rest of the Board agreed in the summer of 1966 and the Hubbell Trading Post started to fulfill its role as a living monument. To the end of his life, Danson considered this one of his greatest accomplishments.

A major milestone in Danson's life occurred at the October, 1958, meeting of the Museum's Board of Trustees. Dr. Colton formally submitted his resignation and recommended Assistant Director Edward B. Danson as his successor. Colton called Danson "well qualified to take over the operation of the Museum and Research Center."

Although Colton's retirement was long expected, the event did have its share of surprises for Harold and Mary-Russell Colton. At the board's formal dinner, Danson announced that he had raised the $50,000 needed to add a long-desired ethnology wing onto the main Museum building.

The announcement was made in the Museum's special exhibit hall, decorated with Danson's other surprise. He had succeeded in acquiring for the Museum a part of the Gladwin collection, valued at over $30,000. At his instructions, Museum Curator Barton Wright, using the rugs from the Gladwin col-

Pottery Conference at Museum of Northern Arizona's Research Center, Danson in foreground

The Gladwin Collection on display at Museum's Board of Trustees' dinner honoring Dr. Colton on the day he announced his retirement as Director, 1958

lection, plus their fine collection of Indian jewelry, decorated
the special exhibit gallery like an opulent trading post. Rugs
hung from the beamed ceiling. They covered the walls and were
stacked around the stage. The floor of the stage was strewn with
the large collection of Indian silver from the Gladwins. Needless
to say, the Coltons and all of the Board and guests were over-
whelmed by the wonder of that room and the curator's work.

That evening, Danson had shown that he could raise funds,
bring an important collection to the Museum and put on a good
show. Ned Danson formally became director of the Museum of
Northern Arizona on January 1, 1959.

Passing the torch. Drs. Harold Colton and Ned Danson in the Museum of North-
ern Arizona's Research Center pottery collection, 1958

CHAPTER FOUR

CHALLENGES & OPPORTUNITIES
Director of the Museum of Northern Arizona
1959 - 1975

In its new director, the Museum had acquired not only a scientist, but someone who had been learning the skills of an administrator since childhood. As a young man, Ned Danson had observed the ways his father, and later his uncle, ran the Kemper-Thomas Company. In his teens, he experienced how Irving Johnson captained the *Yankee* effectively, maintaining comity over eighteen months living in close quarters. During World War II on Bougainville Island, Danson dealt with leadership both good and bad. As a student and professor, he had learned much from Emil Haury about running a museum, a university department with faculty from many disciplines and a summer field school for college students. Over the years, Ned Danson melded this knowledge with a talent for charming people and maintaining relationships that helped him get things done.

In his new position, Danson evaluated the strengths and weaknesses of the Museum he was now leading. Its major strengths included the unique vision of an institution that "encouraged the study of science and art in Northern Arizona;" its connections with Native peoples and the trust that had developed between them over the years; the Museum's tradition of exhibiting "ideas, not things;" the buildings themselves; and MNA's reputation for doing excellent scientific research, the results of which it made available through its publications.

But Danson also saw the Museum's weaknesses. Some of the buildings that the Museum's founders had planned remained unbuilt. Most of the facilities for visiting scientists were inadequate, some even being roughly converted chicken coops. The full-time scientific staff was small, and some of the curators were in Flagstaff only for the summer months. Salaries for the scientists—including the director—were low. Danson knew that he must not only manage the expected growth of the Museum but be "opportunistic" in taking advantage of unexpected projects that came his way.

Even the rapid growth in collections created a problem. Inadequate storage space and insufficient staffing led to collections that were poorly organized and often stored in a manner that risked their being damaged.

Finances remained one of the largest problems. Funded by a mix of membership fees, gifts, grants and the profits from its publications, the Museum was just breaking even. Much of the money came as grants tied to specific projects, and grants for general operations were few. At the end of his second year, the Director reported to the Museum's members:

> The Museum is spending all of its income. Perhaps some might feel that financial and operational curtailments were indicated. But this is not possible, for the inevitable result would be the withering away of the Institution. Expansion of activities is essential to continued life, expansion not in every direction perhaps, but certainly in the . . . main fields of interest to this Institution.

"We must increase our endowments," Danson wrote, "to enable us to increase our staff . . . department budgets, and increase our salary standards." During the Colton years, the Museum had depended largely on the generosity of the extended Colton family and a few of their friends. Danson brought in new donors and encouraged the growing group of Museum members to increase their level of support. He also encouraged "the staff and other scientists to apply for grants from foundations." Although initially wary of applying for government grants, fearful that strings would be attached, he put aside his concerns as the years progressed and competitive opportunities to fund specific projects arose.

While dealing with the finances was a duty, one of the pleasures Danson found in his job came from mentoring interested young people of all ages. In 1959, an elementary school teacher and entomologist from Southern Arizona led a children's science program at the Museum. "Ned saw the importance," the teacher wrote, "of showing appreciation for the children's efforts that summer when he gave us the space in the Museum to exhibit their work. No one else ever thought of making that gesture." A member of the Arizona Academy of Science, Danson began working with Flagstaff's Junior Academy of Science group, led by a local junior high school science teacher. In 1960, the Museum leased a piece of land to the Junior Academy, and the students put up a small laboratory building on the Museum campus. Some high school students volunteered in the summers, helping archaeologists excavate ruins and working with the Research Center's botanist and geologist. Some students at the Academy formed lasting bonds with the Museum, donating works of art to MNA later in life.

William "Bill" Lipe, a summer assistant at the Museum in 1957, and later assistant director, wrote:

> I suspect most young people who were associated with the Museum in the Danson era found it a formative experience. . . . Ned, in his ebullient way, created the encouraging atmosphere that made us feel we were part of a team and that we had what it took to make worthwhile contributions. Furthermore, Ned loved the Southwest and its people, cultures, and history, and he loved to help young people discover these things as well. I'll

always remember a trip I took with him early in my intern summer, and his pleasure in introducing me to wonderful places and people: Betatakin and the Park Service ranger there, Art White; Hubbell Trading Post and Mrs. Hubbell, who was still running it; the Hopi Mesas and some of the Hopi artists.

Although Danson was now Director of the Museum of Northern Arizona, Dr. Colton's influence remained strong. Colton served as President of the Board of Trustees, and weekly meetings between the two men, in Danson's words, "continued until Colton's death . . . and our relationship became like father and son. It was a weekly meeting I looked forward to and enjoyed." At those meetings, they discussed the progress Danson was making at the Museum as it grew.

The number of people working at the Museum increased dramatically over Danson's first few years as director. Summer assistants increased almost four-fold. Funded primarily by the Glen Canyon Project and other salvage archaeology contracts, the year-round archaeology staff increased. Danson added a full-time curator of geology, former summer assistant William "Bill" Breed, and filled other gaps in the staff. The number of independent researchers also grew. Meteorologists, led by Vincent Schaefer from the State University of New York, Albany, began atmospheric studies focusing on thunderstorm development over the San Francisco Peaks. The Museum also attracted a number of volunteers from the community, including neighbor Jane Metzger and Hamilton Parker "Ham" Hamilton, who had been involved in developing the Polaroid process, and who had chosen to retire to Flagstaff, in part, because of the Museum. Ham and his wife Dilly expanded and organized the Photography Department.

Despite the changes at MNA, the Museum community still retained a family atmosphere. In addition to their Christmas Party, the Dansons hosted a summer party for the summer

Ned Danson and Harold Colton at Wupatki National Monument

Ned and Jessica Danson with Hamilton Parker "Ham" Hamilton at Navajo Show

assistants and scientists doing research at the Museum. The Danson family also enjoyed entertaining world-famous scientists and authors who visited the Museum, including Theodosius Dobzhansky, a prominent geneticist and evolutionary biologist, and renowned British author J. B. Priestly, who had traveled to the Museum with his wife, archaeologist Jacquetta Hawkes. Jan remembered that, after dinner at the Homestead, Priestly taught the family an English drinking game called "Cardinal Puff," in which players were required to repeat a series of words and gestures of increasing complexity. Priestly set a sum of money on the Dansons' living room floor and promised to give it to anyone who could repeat his gestures and words precisely the first time. He kept his money. Jan spent the night practicing the game so she could share it with her high school English literature class.

Ned Danson loved to look at unspoiled nature. He and Jessica both enjoyed watching sunsets. Sometimes, instead of sitting on the Homestead's porch, they took their children and guests seventy-five miles north to the Grand Canyon to watch the moment from one of the most stunning places in the world. But they did not have to go that far to see beauty. Danson often took the family to the San Francisco Peaks, sacred ground to Hopi, Navajo, Zuni, and other Native peoples and just a few miles away from the Museum. There they had picnics on grassy meadows, surrounded by groves of white-barked aspen trees, watching the sun set behind the rows of mountains receding into the distance.

To Danson, the drive to these spots was as pleasurable as the picnic itself. In 1959, the car-lover purchased his first Mercedes Benz. The car carried the sense of class and style that Danson embodied so easily; it was a perfect fit. For the rest of his life, even after he stopped driving, Danson would own a Mercedes.

Playing games, reading, picnicking on the San Francisco Peaks and hosting cocktail and dinner parties—these were some of the things the Danson family did for entertainment. The family had no television set until after their children left home. Aside from visits to friends or to the Lungés in California, Ted would have to wait years to get a good look at the medium that would play a big part in his later life. Flagstaff had one movie theater and one drive-in, which was open only in the summer. Once, when the family was bored, Jan and Ted talked their parents into going to a movie. Their father did not approve of the free sexual behavior of the characters on the screen and ordered the whole family to leave. Jan remembered walking past her high school classmates, feeling humiliated, as her father muttered about how awful it was that people made such movies.

The Dansons often visited Jessica's parents and the Lungés in Pasadena, California, over Christmas or New Years. In return, they hosted the Lungés in the summer. Eileen marveled at all the work her sister was doing. "She was a hostess and a 'motel' maid and a caterer," Eileen said. "She would prepare the accommodations for guests, research associates and summer interns, cleaning, dusting, and making sure all was comfortable for them. . . . She was gracious and welcoming to visiting scientists and students and made them feel they were a part of the Museum family."

A Museum employee later wrote, "When considering Jessica's role during Ned's tenure as director, what better title than 'Associate to the Director!' Even though Jess did not have an assistant or a salary or a budget, she served in a very professional capacity at the Museum."

While the sisters stayed in Flagstaff, Jeffrey often joined Ned on excursions to the reservations and elsewhere across Northern Arizona. Even when it was technically business travel, such as a collecting trip for one of the shows, Danson often stopped along the road to share a particularly picturesque view with Lungé. "I told him to ask me to stop whenever he saw a mesa or a cliff, a tree or a vista he wanted to sketch," Danson said. "Jeff opened my eyes to the beauty of this part of the world. I knew I loved it—but with his artist's eye he would show me things I would have ignored—colors I hadn't seen."

Ted and Ned Danson with Jeffrey Lungé at a picnic on the San Francisco Peaks

Home from the Sing, *watercolor by Jeffrey Lungé*

Jan remembered one trip that both families took to the North Rim of the Grand Canyon. On the drive home, they passed Navajo riders returning from a sing, a scene which inspired Jeffrey to paint one of his first of many watercolors of Navajo horsemen.

The Haurys were also frequent guests at the Homestead, and the Dansons made trips to Tucson to see them and other friends. In December, 1959, the Haurys and Dansons planned a trip to the American Anthropological Association meetings in Mexico City. But Emil Haury fell ill and was unable to attend. So Ned invited Loren Haury to accompany his family to Mexico City, followed by a trip to Yucatan with Jo Brew and an archaeologist who had excavated a Mayan temple there.

In Yucatan, Loren and the Dansons celebrated New Year's Eve at Chichen Itza and the next day traveled to Uxmal. That night Jan, Loren and Ted decided to climb the Temple of the Magician in the light of a full moon. In this ancient, romantic ruin, Jan and Loren—long past the days at Point of Pines when she was a "tad" and he a "frog"—began to fall in love. While being able to spend so much time together was changing Jan and Loren's lives, that night nearly ended Ted's. As they were climbing down the temple's steep steps, Ted, not looking where he was going, almost fell into a deep hole archaeologists had dug to gain access to the inner chamber. Loren saw what was about to happen and grabbed Ted before he could step into the pit, likely saving his future brother-in-law's life.

At the end of the school year in 1961, the Danson family reached a turning point. Jan graduated from high school, and Ted completed the eighth grade. Jan was accepted at Wellesley College in Massachusetts. Ted was admitted to Kent, an Episcopal boy's boarding school in Connecticut. In September, both of the Danson children left the Homestead for the East. Jessica said she felt like she was "flying on one wing."

But, as director, Ned Danson was soaring. One of his most important innovations at this time was creation of the Collector's Club. On his trips out of town, Danson, who enjoyed looking in galleries, sometimes found a work of art that he thought should be in the Museum's collection. But he was rarely able to purchase it. "No private museum," Danson stated in his 1962 Annual Report, "has enough unallocated money . . . to enable the Director to take advantage of all the opportunities that come his way to purchase collections. The establishment in the past year of the Collectors Club with 24 members was an accomplishment of decided importance." Club members each donated one hundred dollars a year, making $2,400 available to the Director to purchase unexpected finds for the Museum. The first year, Danson purchased an 1880 painting of the Kaibab Plateau and an 1869 watercolor of the Hopi village of Walpi.

In part, due to those purchases, Ned Danson was pleased to announce that year that, "At long last, the Museum's art collections are growing." A total of nine paintings had been acquired. And through his outreach, Danson continued to secure more. He had spent many years getting to know Katherine Harvey, granddaughter of Fred Harvey, whose tour of the Southwest Danson had taken as a boy. In 1963, she died and left a collection of Indian art to the Museum. The collection contained more than one hundred paintings, including watercolors by Hopi artist Fred Kabotie and Apache Allan Houser.

Sometimes, one acquisition—even a temporary one—led to another. "When I was collecting paintings and etchings by [George Elbert] Burr—an Arizona artist of the 1920s/1930s for a Museum exhibition," Danson recalled, "I went to see [the] president of the Valley National Bank [in Phoenix] to see if I could borrow [theirs]. He agreed and told me that the Smurthwaites had a shop out at the Arizona Biltmore Hotel and had a large collection of Burr etchings and that they might loan some of their collection." Danson went to the Biltmore at once, and the Smurthwaites agreed to loan a few of their etchings to him. Danson considered the Burr show to be a success, but just as important to him, "That was the beginning of a long and good

Clay Lockett and Ned Danson at the Research Center

friendship," with the Smurthwaites. Carolann Smurthwaite and her mother often contacted Danson to tell him about Southwestern paintings he might want to purchase for the Museum. Years later, at Carolann Smurthwaite's death, she left her Burr collection to the Museum.

As the Museum's collections expanded, so did the number of visitors, due in part to the road past the Museum becoming one of the main highways to the Grand Canyon. To further meet the needs of the additional visitors, Danson enlisted his old friend Clay Lockett to create a shop in the Museum's main building. Half owned by the Lockett family and half by the Museum, it opened in 1963 and began providing a year-round market for Native American wares. "This," Danson explained, "will fill a long realized need, not only for Museum visitors, but also for the people of the area. Only books and Indian crafted material will be handled in the shop, and since Mr. Lockett is recognized as one of the leading Indian Arts and Crafts dealers in the Southwest, we feel the Museum has made a significant step forward." Another reason for opening the Museum Shop was to provide an outlet for Southwestern Native American arts and crafts during the winter season, when few tourists visited the reservations. In 1967, the Hopis brought in $7,000 worth of katsina dolls to the shop, providing a steady income for the carvers. Profits from the sales also helped finance the Museum. Eventually, the Museum bought out the Lockett family, acquiring complete ownership of the store.

Although the Museum's scientific research tended to focus on the past, an unexpected opportunity let Danson and the Museum help America enter the Space Age. As the volcanic rock around Flagstaff was deemed to be a suitable approximation of the moon's surface, the United States Geological Survey Astrogeology Research Program wanted to establish a laboratory in the area. Because the Geological Survey said that it would take considerable time to fund and build a lab of their own, in the spring of 1962 the astrogeologists asked Flagstaff's Lowell Observatory, a world famous center for astronomical research, if they could use its facilities in the interim. The Observatory and several other Flagstaff institutions were unable to commit their space at that time.

Soon after, Danson recalled, "I watched three men approach the Research Center. They discussed with me the need for space for a small number of scientists who would be working on projects related to the United States efforts to land a space vehicle and men on the moon. . . ." Danson recognized what an opportunity this was for the Museum. "I asked them how much room they needed . . . [and] said I would see what I could do."

The next afternoon, he contacted one of the Museum's regular donors and asked for a loan. The following day, Danson reported, "a check was in the mail." He presented a plan to the USGS to build a new wing at the Research Center for their use. The USGS agreed to pay rent on the space, enabling the Museum to pay off the loan. Construction began within a month.

As soon as the building was complete, the astrogeologists began working day and night under the leadership of Dr. Eugene Shoemaker, father of astrogeology, making lunar maps and, beginning in 1963, giving geological training to fifty-four Apollo Astronauts at Sunset and Meteor Craters near Flagstaff. After several years, the USGS's new Flagstaff facilities were completed, freeing the additional space for Museum scientists. But the relationships established with the astrogeologists endured. Eugene Shoemaker and his wife, Carolyn, remained close to the Museum, both later serving terms on the Board of Trustees. And because of the Museum's cooperation with Shoemaker and the Geological Survey, MNA became one of the first museums outside of Washington, D.C., to display a moon rock brought back to earth by the Apollo astronauts.

Danson continued to use many methods to help the institution grow. The early 1960s saw significant growth in both full time staff, which doubled between 1961 and 1964, and in independent researchers. One key method of attracting independent researchers was hosting conferences, four in 1964 alone. These conferences ranged in subject from the geology of the Colorado Plateau to the study of traditional prehistoric ceramics and the ecology of the nearby San Francisco Peaks. The ecology conference was held on the 75th anniversary of research by C. Hart Merriam on the San Francisco Peaks, which led to his development of the concept of ecological life zones. "All of these functions added to the prestige of the Museum," Danson wrote in one of his annual reports, "and . . . there are, each year, more and more requests for permission to do research and to work at the Research Center as a result of conferences."

But not all of the conferences went smoothly. One year, when the Museum was hosting the Pecos Conference for Southwestern field archaeologists, the Dansons invited forty of the attendees to the Homestead for nightcaps. They went to bed about 1:30 AM. Danson recalled what happened next:

> At 3:30, the hospital called to say that one of our staff
> had injured herself; and her husband, who had driven her
> to the hospital, had fainted dead away and had a concus-

sion. Jess insisted that I sleep on while she drove down and got Nina and returned home about 4:30. At 5:15, the El Paso gas-line company decided to blow their new pipes, which they are installing. This sounds exactly as though a jet were going to crash on your house—a jet with full power on, the only difference being that the noise lasts for half an hour. Everyone, including Emil and Hulda, our house guests, sat bolt upright, then rushed around to find out what was going on. Then someone called me and said that this had been planned, which infuriated me, as we had about 100 people sleeping at the camp ground at the Research Center, quite close to the place where they were blowing the pipe. I called up the pipe-line company manager and gave him hell, and jumped in my car and drove up to the camp ground. The people there looked like a bunch of ants running in all directions, everybody trying to find out what . . . was going on.

In 1964, Danson's six-year term on the National Park Service Advisory Board was about to come to an end. Emil Haury was selected to take his seat, one of the few times Danson preceded his mentor at anything. But Danson did not want to leave. Much of the work he had done on the Board involved perusing reports on sites of historical interest, describing their importance and their current condition. In many ways, the reports were like the history books Ned had loved to read all his life. And Danson believed that he and other members soon to leave the Board had developed expertise which could still be of use to the National Park Service. "I was talking," Danson wrote, "with some other members whose term was coming to an end. We went to see Secretary of the Interior Stewart Udall." They suggested that he establish an Advisory Council made up of retired members of the Board. "The Council members could advise but did not have a vote. This idea was accepted and lasted until Ronald Reagan's term as President." Danson's suggestion enabled him to spend almost twenty more years doing a job he loved.

In early 1965, Danson looked back at five years of his directorship and reported on the progress that he had overseen. In science, he said, "Suffice it to say here that all departments have grown in staff and number of research projects." As far as buildings were concerned, "The original set of plans for the Museum included sections [not complete in 1959]. They are now built." And the "cottages, workshops, laboratories, houses for staff, and other buildings, as well as the grounds, drives, and paths—all needed attention. All have been improved." But additional building had not kept up with the growth in the number of scientists applying to use the Research Center. "We must now turn down requests for space and housing that come in from scientists and institutions throughout the country," he noted.

Danson enumerated other changes to the Museum:

> Where we had one anthropologist and two summer assistants in Anthropology in 1959, last year we had six on the staff, four of them full time, and sixteen summer and special assistants.
>
> We now give six summer grant-in-aids to graduate students each year to work on projects we would like to see studied which are acceptable to the student's major professor. In 1959, this program hadn't yet begun.
>
> Last year, there were three field schools operating out of the Museum, and twenty-two independent scientists worked at the Museum on their own projects. In 1959, there were sixteen scientists and one field school. . . .
>
> In 1959, we had one contract for research. In 1965, we had twelve contracts that amounted to over $100,000. This trend is a growing one.
>
> In 1959, 22,290 people visited the Museum. . . . Almost 55,000 people saw the Museum in 1965.

All of these factors were feeding on themselves. Larger collections and a bigger library lured more researchers. The presence of so many researchers encouraged the region's Federal land management agencies to house their collections of Southwest artifacts at the Research Center.

The goals Danson set forth for the coming years included his reminder that everyone in the Museum had to be "opportunistic." He encouraged staff scientists and visiting researchers to apply for grants "to enable the departments to continue the research programs they started under our meager funds," and he sought to increase the Museum's endowment.

"And finally," he wrote, "we must encourage the local schools to make use of our facilities and the townspeople to realize that the Museum is for them—that it is . . . a place where ideas can be seen and things can be studied in a quiet oasis."

Although Watson Smith had been right that Danson would never be a professor again after joining the Museum, this did not mean he couldn't be a mentor or facilitate education. "The Museum in my mind," Danson wrote, "is an educational institution and has been since its founding." In 1966, he noted that more than four hundred students have studied under the auspices of the Museum since its founding. "They learned that geology, archaeology, and biology are not totally concerned with marvelous and exciting 'days in the field' and that there were more days in the lab that were, in many respects, filled with tedious and painstaking preparation, analysis, and study. They were taught the specialized techniques of the scientific field of their interest." One college student working at the Museum under a work-study program said, "I've learned more practical knowledge here at the Museum in two years than I have at the university in four."

In a time when it was becoming more important for a scientist to have an advanced degree, Danson took pride in the fact that from 1956-1966, "eight students have received a Ph.D. degree, whose research was sponsored by the Museum."

In 1965, a young man begged Danson for a job at the Museum. At the time, young Steven Carothers had no intention of becoming a scientist. He just wanted work and was given a job at the Museum's front desk on weekends. But because of the Museum's close community, Carothers, in Danson's words, "became interested in biology watching [MNA botanist] Dr. McDougall put the fresh flowers in the botany rack in the Museum every morning." Danson encouraged his interest, which expanded to include the study of mammals and birds. In 1968, only a few years after asking for a part time job, Carothers earned a Master's degree and became the Museum's Assistant Curator of Zoology. He received his Ph.D. in 1974 from the University of Illinois and later founded SWCA Environmental Consultants.

"One of the good things that happens to any person in charge of an institution," Danson wrote, "is seeing a person one has befriended as a student grow in stature and responsibility. Steven Carothers is one such person."

Carothers, for his part, wrote that "in my life, Ned was MNA." He recalled that, "Long after Ned left the directorship of the institution, and long after he was no longer my direct supervisor, he continued to 'boss' me around. 'Cut your hair, young man, you will never amount to much with that long hair.' This was almost one of the last things he said to me. . . . He was perfectly aware that I was no longer a young man, that the hair he wanted cut had been gray and white for decades, he just liked being my boss, and his 'orders' were his way of telling me I still mattered to him."

Bill Lipe wrote that Danson "delighted in sharing his enthusiasm with students and staff, and especially in finding ways to give young people a good start on their careers."

"That was Ned," Carothers said, "we really did matter to him in a personal way."

Carothers had chosen a growing field to study. While most departments at the Museum were expanding at the time, Biology and Geology were leading the way. The number of biologists working at the Museum increased from two to nineteen.

Dedication of the Lionel F. Brady Geology Building, 1967. (Left to right) Ned Danson, Harold Colton, William Breed, Richard Wilson and Willie Coin

Dr. Edwin "Ned" Colbert in his office in the Research Center's Brady Building

And in 1967, a new geology building was completed, named after the late Major Brady, to house the growing department. "There is no doubt," Danson wrote, "that the research facilities in the new building will enable us to attract . . . new scientists of repute. . . ."

That year, Danson wrote, "It was a great pleasure . . . to have Dr. Keith Runcorn return to the Museum . . . to continue his work." The work Runcorn had done at the Museum, studying the paleomagnetism of rocks in the Flagstaff area, had borne fruit. Magnetic signatures left in volcanic rocks provided evidence that the continents were slowly moving. This research helped change the idea of continental drift, once disparaged as an impractical fantasy, into a viable, scientific theory.

But Runcorn's work alone was not sufficient to prove the hypothesis of continental drift. In 1968, the Museum again played a small role in trying to prove this hypothesis, and the help came from another man named "Ned."

Edwin "Ned" Colbert had been a paleontologist at Columbia University and the American Museum of Natural History. In the mid-1960s, Colbert was preparing to retire. He had previously spent time at the Research Center rewriting a textbook, giving Danson the chance to get to know him and recognize his talents. In him, Danson saw another opportunity for the Museum, due in part to the availability of office and lab space in the new geology building.

"Dr. Edward (Ned) Danson, director of the museum," Colbert wrote in his autobiography, "suggested to me one day when he was in New York on a museum business trip that if . . . I wished to settle in Flagstaff, the museum there could accommodate me with a place to work."

In 1968, Ned Colbert came to the Museum of Northern Arizona and within two years was appointed Curator of Vertebrate Paleontology. The previous year, Colbert and the Museum's Curator of Geology, Bill Breed, had joined an expedition to Antarctica to search for fossil evidence for continental drift.

On the expedition, Colbert recognized that the fossilized bones of a small reptile they had excavated from Antarctic sandstone was a *Lystrosaurus*, the same species as one he had found in South Africa on an earlier trip. This showed that Antarctica and Africa had once been connected and provided a key piece of evidence that persuaded scientists of the validity of continental drift, one of the more important theories of the 20th century.

In a *New York Times* article, eminent geologist and early Antarctic explorer Dr. Laurence M. Gould said that he "considered the find not only the most important fossil ever found in Antarctica but one of the truly great fossil finds of all times."

But scientists weren't the only people Danson brought to the Museum. To him, art was something not merely to be collected but to be studied and encouraged. Besides driving his artist brother-in-law, Jeffrey Lungé, around the Southwest, Danson opened the Museum's collections to Lungé for study, allowing him to add authenticity to his work. Danson also cultivated relationships with other artists, including Don Percival, a painter from Santa Barbara, who illustrated *A Navajo Sketchbook* with text written by Clay Lockett. In his correspondence with Percival, Danson sent him a list of paintings he wished to add to the Museum's collection. Included were works from prominent Southwestern artists like Maynard Dixon, Gunnar Widforss, and Louis Akin, as well as works by Percival himself. In a letter in which Danson told Percival that the board had named him a "research associate in art," he added, "I also should say how much I appreciate your suggesting to Harry James that the beautiful painting you did for him . . . be left in his will to the museum. I consider this your first major work as a research associate."

Ned Danson also encouraged budding artists to pursue their passion. John Farnsworth, a staff member at the Museum, remembered a 1966 conversation with Danson. "The Museum Director took me aside, one day, and said, 'Your mind really isn't on your work here, is it?' 'No Sir,' I answered. 'You'd really rather be painting, wouldn't you?' 'Yes, Sir.' 'Then go paint. And if you stick with it, I think you might be great some day.' Well, that's all I needed to hear. . . . I will forever be grateful."

By cultivating relationships with both artists and collectors, Danson was well placed to take advantage of opportunities for new acquisitions for the Museum. He had already established a relationship with the Harvey family, having secured Katherine Harvey's collection of Indian paintings for the Museum. But her grandfather Fred Harvey's diverse collection of Western arts and crafts remained warehoused in Albuquerque. In 1963, the Harvey family asked Ned Danson and Clay Lockett to evaluate this collection.

Danson was horrified at what he discovered. "I found that the collection was stored in a small office," he wrote. "I opened one drawer and beads from a Plains Indian beaded jacket popped out. It had been crammed into the drawer too tightly. There were big pots with metates [grinding stones] in them, pot after pot after pot stacked up. . . ." Rare items had started to decay. The building was a severe fire risk. Danson wrote to a member of the Harvey family about his concerns. He argued that the collection had to be moved as quickly as possible.

In his letter, Danson listed several possibilities for what to do with the collection, including splitting it up, selling some (one of the worst options, in his opinion), placing them in private but protected storage, or giving them to a single museum, such as the Museum of Northern Arizona, and providing funding for their upkeep. In response to his letter, the collection was transferred temporarily to storage at the Grand Canyon, but a permanent home needed to be found. The Harvey family put together a committee to explore their options and invited Danson to join.

Acquiring the Fred Harvey collection could have been a great feather in the cap of the Museum and its director. But upon examining the situation thoroughly, Danson felt that the Museum of Northern Arizona could not handle the entire collection without additional funding, which was not being offered. Rather than advocate for it to be split and given to different museums, including MNA—an acceptable, but in Danson's mind, inferior option—he put the needs of the collection first. "It didn't take long," he recalled, for the committee, "to come to the decision that the collection should go to the Heard Museum. It was too diverse a collection to belong to the Museum of Northern Arizona."

But Ned Danson didn't spend all his time on such serious matters. Not even he, as a trained anthropologist, wanted to keep his mind on his work all the time. As director, he corresponded frequently with Emil Haury, Watson Smith, Arnie Withers and other archaeologists on subjects ranging from the dating of ceramics, to the definition of cultural groups and even whom to hire for various positions. But often in these serious correspondences, especially with Smith and Withers, Ned and his colleagues engaged in play.

Arnie Withers, recalling Ned Danson's elegant attire, even in the field, wrote a memorandum about how to dress for a dig at Point of Pines, using a photograph of his old college classmate as an illustration. "Tweed Jacket," he advised, adding, " . . . remember the nights are apt to be cool . . . . Color should be dark as cleaning establishments are limited in number, and cleaning services often require two to three days. . . ." In addition to the pressed flannel trousers, oxford cloth shirt, white shoes, and crew haircut, Withers reminded people to bring "one pointing finger," warning "don't get the type which is welded to hand" and promising "other tools furnished if needed." Withers had the memorandum posted on the Anthropology bulletin board at the University of Arizona.

Danson, upon learning of this post, wrote to Withers to add his own expert advice and correct some of Withers' mistakes.

I seriously doubt that my former opinion of you was correct. . . . I had thought you to be observant, but your remarks, A to G, under "What to Bring" are full of serious errors which denote a lack of powers of observa-

TO APPLICANTS
for
UNIVERSITY OF ARIZONA ARCHAEOLOGICAL FIELD SCHOOL
POINT*OF*PINES
NANTACK RIDGE
SAN CARLOS APACHE INDIAN RESERVE
SAN CARLOS,ARIZONA

WELCOME ALL!

Note 1: What to bring.
a. Tweed jacket (remember, the nights are apt to be
cool; elevation, remember, is 6000'. Color
should be dark as cleaning establishments are
limited in number, and cleaning services often
require two to three days)

b. Pressed flannel trousers (as illustrated).
Experience has shown that it is better
to have the crease sewn in as cleaning establishments etc. (see above)

c. One white oxford cloth shirt (illust/
Come to think of it, better
bring two, as occasionally
we have Sat. night Devil
Dances.

d. One necktie (as illust).
Preferably plain and
in a subdued color.
(The natives
sometimes re-
act violently
to harsh,
clashing hue:
And, anyway,
we like these
better at
Harvard.)

e. One pr. white buck
shoes (as illust.)
These are sturdy, and we
have found them easier to clean
inside than high-topped shoes or boots. Rubber
soles are preferred as they reduce the chance of
accidents in climbing the mess counter in the
dining hall and the enlarged photographic tripod.

f. One crew haircut (as illust.)
Remember, cleaning establishments etc. (see above).
Bring two if there is room in your duffle.

g. One pointing finger (as illust.)
Do not get the type which is welded to hand.
This tool is essential for pointing to arrowheads
and work accomplished (and has many other uses in
a mixed camp.) Other tools furnished if needed.
Note 2: If these requirements present any difficulties,
come as you are.

tion. Now, friend (?), an ability to observe is a highly important part of an archaeologist's equipment. . . . The jacket should be cut only by Brooks brothers and should be of a thick luxurious home-spun. None of these ready-mades. . . . White Buck Shoes—Are actually Clark's Desert Boots, of British manufacture.

Another humorous exchange among anthropologists involved an examination of the word "ickle," an Old English term for "icicle." After receiving an article on the subject from Watson Smith, Danson proposed that there might be more kinds of "ickles" besides icicles. "I have . . . seen many ickles," he wrote to Smith. "This morning early it was cold and on my way downtown I developed a nose-ickle. I might add that nose-ickles are apt to tickle and that my nose-ickle tickled which caused a sneezicle to form. I rather like that word. I think we can do all kinds of things with it."

Smith replied, "I am very happy that you are an ickle-dropper, and I have filed with the general archives your contributions, which I think are of great value."

"Ickle" later provided the basis for Danson's title in the "Sacred Order of Omphalopsychites," a more formalized forum for levity among this group of Southwestern anthropologists. Named after a mystical Eastern Orthodox sect that practiced navel gazing, the order had been co-founded and led by Emil Haury (who held the position of "Chief Gazer"). Joining after its creation, Danson was made the "Omnipotent Omphalopsickle" and took his place among such fellow members as Watson Smith ("the Research Hesychast") and Jo Brew of the "Boston Navel District." A few non-anthropologists were allowed to join the group, such as Emil Haury's secretary ("the Keeper of the Lint") and Dorothy Pollock ("the Looker Into").

At gatherings, this group engaged in exaggerated rituals, involving navel brushes and ornaments such as a "Golden Navel Salt Cellar," which came with a free box of salt. Between meetings,

NATIONAL ORDER OF OMPHALOPSYCHITES

Contemplation

Perception   Transcendence

Ex Umbilicum Fraternitas

Letterhead of the Omphalopsychites, designed by Watson Smith

Chief Gazer Haury wrote to his colleagues letters that, abandoning his usual, simple and businesslike style, included sentences such as: "You will note by the enclosed letter . . . that I, as Chief Gazer, have been fully contemplative, perceptive, and transcendent, and have carried out the wishes of the Order," and "In the past few months your serious contemplative moods . . . and the transcendent quality of your nature have been carefully observed. . . ." The Omnipotent Omphalopsickle and his other fellow members responded in kind.

The pleasure Danson took in various forms of humor was clear to those who knew his memorable laughter. Ray and Molly Thompson wrote that, "No one could pack so much meaning into a laugh as Ned Danson. Whether it was a quiet chuckle or a hearty guffaw, his laugh injected something special into any and every situation. His laughter could be quietly cheerful, enthusiastically joyful, raucously lecherous, mischievously silly, properly stern, [or] unconsciously cynical. . . ." He was as eager to laugh "when the joke was on him," as when it was not. And the Thompsons recalled that "His laughter was one of the strong suits in his unique kind of social interaction that enabled him to accomplish so much for the Museum of Northern Arizona."

Another activity that gave Ned Danson pleasure was traveling across the Colorado Plateau. His role at the Museum gave him an opportunity to visit dig sites, explore national parks and monuments, and observe changes being brought about by Glen Canyon Dam and other projects. He loved the adventure of being in the wild, the beauty he found there and the time he shared on those trips with old friends.

While Danson was a member of the National Park Service Advisory Board, photographers Ham and Dilly Hamilton and river-runner Bates Wilson encouraged him to help preserve the prehistory and intricately carved canyons and mesas of the Canyonlands wilderness, which was in danger of being mined for uranium and flooded by a proposed dam where the Colorado and Green rivers joined. With Secretary of Interior Stewart Udall's support, Congress passed a law in 1964, making Canyonlands a national park. Four years later, Danson was able to enjoy the land he had helped preserve. "In September," Danson wrote, "Jess and I joined Emil, . . . [Ham and Dilly] Hamilton, [son] Ted and Bates Wilson for . . . 5 heavenly days of camping in Canyonlands." That same month, he spent three days touring through Betatakin, Kayenta, Monument Valley and Canyon de Chelly.

Danson also took the time to visit archaeological sites being excavated by MNA staff or to follow up on leads about possible new excavations. For the most part, he had no role in the field work itself. But there were exceptions. In 1960, along with another archaeologist, he participated in a salvage archaeology survey for a railroad right-of-way north of Prescott. And after a woman reported finding early man spear points near St. John's, Arizona, Danson and another staff member visited her home. "Recently," he wrote his mother, "she found a large site on which she had collected Folsum [sic], Pinto Basin and Silver Lake like points — over 50 from the one site. . . . She took us out to see the site and we collected there for 2 hours." He noted that there were eight other sites nearby and decided to return in the summer "to do more testing. . . ."

Anthropology remained one of Danson's passions. In the annual reports he wrote to Museum members, Anthropology was the department he discussed in the most detail. But the bulk of his work remained the administration of an institution dedicated, not just to anthropology, but to a variety of disciplines, and it was to that job that he dedicated most of his efforts.

The years from 1965 to 1969 proved to be the high watermark of Danson's tenure at the Museum. During this time, yearly attendance increased by nearly 12,000 to over 65,000 visitors. In the winter of 1967, "for the first time in [Danson's] memory, every usable house that can [be] heated during the winter, and has indoor plumbing, is being used" by staff and the many visiting scientists. The same thing happened the following year. "Not a month passes," Danson wrote, "that some scientist does not come to me with ideas, good ideas in most instances, of how the Museum could help in this or that research project. There are so many things to do and so little time. . . ."

To help get these things done, Danson took advantage of Lyndon Johnson's Great Society work-study program, which provided funding for low-income students at Northern Arizona University and other colleges to work at the Museum in both research and support roles. "These students are an important asset to the Museum," Danson reported, "and I am happy that we are continuing to work with the university in this program, as it has enabled us to complete many jobs that would otherwise have to wait."

But funding for the Great Society programs started to wane at the end of the 1960s. At least one Museum scientist started to supplement his income by lecturing part-time at Flagstaff's Northern Arizona University.

Fortunately, the Museum's reputation allowed it to eke out a few more years of work-study students, becoming the only non-university institution still to be allowed to use NAU students. Around this time, a former staff member recalls going to see the director in his office, but being told by his secretary that he was not in. Money from grants had not come in on time, she explained. There was not enough available to make the month's payroll, so Danson had gone to the bank to withdraw some of his own funds to pay the staff until the grant money arrived.

Danson also faced a more personal problem. Since the time his children left home, he had been struggling to give up smoking his two packs of cigarettes a day. Like many smokers, he pretended to be more successful than he was. Long periods of abstinence were followed by relapses. To hide these relapses, he started chewing mint drops. Jessica often wondered why he was doing this, but her husband was always able to guide the conversation away from the topic.

Another health problem Danson faced had its roots in his service in World War II. The substandard dental work he had received in the Navy had led to severe dental problems. He already had a few false teeth, but his remaining teeth were so damaged that he asked his dentist to remove them all at once. Until he received his new teeth, his usual broad smile was covered by his hand while working. For the rest of his life, he used a full set of dentures. But playful Ned Danson did more than simply use them to chew. He developed the ability to push the lower plate of dentures partially out of his mouth, then to pull them back in again with his tongue. He enjoyed surprising and amusing children with this trick, occasionally suggesting to those too young to know better that they should go to their father "and ask him to do it." Some of the children did just that.

While Danson was usually charming, he could become suddenly angry. His daughter remembered numerous arguments she had with him when she was a teenager, in which she pointed out that he had become angry, only for him to pound on the table and shout, "I'm not angry!"

One of the most memorable times Danson lost his temper occurred when he took a large group of Museum guests out to a Flagstaff restaurant for dinner. He and his guests were forced to wait a long time for a table, and Danson saw others, apparently arriving without reservations, being shown to tables ahead of his party.

Enraged at the presumed slight, Danson went to the person at the front desk to complain, and said, "I'm not just an ordinary tourist, you know!"

But many of the people with him misheard. They thought he had declared "I'm not just an ordinary turtle!" Danson's anger cooled quickly, as it always did, and the incident led to years of his receiving turtle-themed gifts with good humor.

Ted also faced his father's anger. During his rebellious teen years, when he was home for the summer from school, someone working at the Museum introduced him and his friends to Edward Abbey's novel, *The Monkey Wrench Gang*, in which activists sabotaged property belonging to people they believed were destroying the environment.

This inspired Ted and his friends to cut down billboards along nearby roads—an irony, since Ted's own grandfather was said to have had a hand in the invention of billboards. Ted and his band snuck out at night to cut the signs down. Soon the local newspaper was reporting their deeds, although the community had no idea who was perpetrating them. However, the fact that a sign promoting the Museum of Northern Arizona had been spared, while two billboards on either side had not, was noted in the article.

While Ted was taking a bath one night, crunched in a bathtub that no longer fit his growing body, his father burst into the room brandishing the newspaper.

"Did you have anything to do with this?" Ned Danson asked his son.

The future Emmy-winning actor put all his nascent skills into shaking his head and saying, "No."

Ned Danson stared at his son for a few moments, then said, "Well, if I ever find that you did it, I will be furious," and left the room. A few seconds later, he pushed the door open again and said that he hoped Ted had cut down a real estate agent's billboard that he particularly disliked.

The mid-1960s was another time of change for Ned Danson and his family. Ned's mother died in 1964, and Jessica's father died a year later. And the Dansons' children were growing up.

Jan graduated from Wellesley College in 1965. That August, for the first time in his career at the Museum, Danson took a lengthy summer vacation. After the Hopi and Navajo Shows were over, Ned joined Jessica, Jan and Ted for a trip to Europe. They spent a long weekend in Austria at the Salzburg Festival with their friends the Megrews, from Boulder, and explored Vienna with a former anthropology student of Danson's from the University of Arizona. Then the family sailed from Venice to Greece to see its ancient ruins. In Athens, they spent a spectacular evening, wandering around the Acropolis in full moonlight. At Pylos, home of Nestor's Palace, a late Bronze Age site made famous in works of Homer, Ned and Jessica visited Watson Smith's goddaughter and her parents, whom Smith had met while helping preserve murals on the palace walls. The trip ended with the family spending a few days in Rome. Ned and Ted left Europe early so Ted could return to Kent for his senior year and Ned, to his duties at the Museum, which Watson Smith had taken over for him in his absence.

Jessica returned to Flagstaff a month later. Always interested in religion, she resumed her responsibilities at the local Episcopal Church as a part of the Altar Guild. As well as entertaining scientists at the Homestead, she also hosted the Bishop of the Diocese of Arizona whenever he came to Flagstaff. And the lure of the landscape brought several religious teachers to Flagstaff, including English author and spiritual retreat leader Sybil Harton, and Nicholas Zernov, a Russian Orthodox layman from Oxford, both of whom led spiritual retreats in the area and stayed at the Homestead. Ned took Sybil Harton on a tour of Hopi country, where she was impressed by the "vast empty quiet of the desert." Harton and Zernov became two of Jessica's spiritual mentors.

In 1966, Ted graduated from Kent and, in the fall, entered Stanford University. His parents drove him to school. One evening on the drive, the Dansons ate dinner in a restaurant. When the check came, Danson pulled his wallet out of the inside pocket of his sports jacket. A pack of cigarettes sailed from his pocket and landed on the table in front of Jessica.

"Ned," Jessica cried in shock, "you've been deceiving me!" Ted sat silent with a smile on his face, watching his father get into trouble.

At Stanford, Ted's life changed when he took an acting class to be close to a girl he liked. He later called his parents to let them know how much he loved acting and said he wanted to pursue it as a career.

Ted later recalled sensing that his father was uncomfortable with the idea, although the precise reason for this was never brought into the open. During his early acting career, Ted felt a persistent aura of negativity and uncertainty. He remembered when his parents came to Stanford to attend one of his student plays, *Sergeant Musgrave's Dance*, in which he was required to kiss an actress. After the performance, his mother showed her usual enthusiasm at his creativity. But his father only said, "The kiss was too loud."

His initial discomfort, however, did not stop Ned Danson from supporting his son financially, as he pursued his dream by transferring to Carnegie Tech in Pittsburg to major in acting. Over time, the tension faded, and Ted recalled with pride that, late in life, his father said to him, "You're a good actor."

Jan, in the meantime, had completed studies for her master's degree in government from the University of Arizona and was preparing to write her thesis. In 1967, she married Loren Haury. Loren was just out of the Navy, having fulfilled his lifelong dream of being a jet pilot, and was about to enter the University of California, San Diego's Ocean Engineering program.

Jan and Loren Haury and their parents at their wedding reception at Clay and Florence Lockett's home in Tucson, Arizona, September 1967

Ned Danson was delighted by this union, as Emil Haury was already his best friend. Danson had known his son-in-law since birth—longer even than he had known Jessica—having been with Haury at the University of Arizona's archaeological field school at Forestdale the night in 1939 when Loren was born.

A few months later, the Dansons celebrated their first Christmas without their daughter. But the Homestead was not empty. In mid-December, heavy snow had begun to fall, and it didn't let up for several weeks. Flagstaff recorded eighty-seven inches of snow over eleven days. So much snow covered the Research Center buildings that the roofs were in danger of collapsing. "Pretty soon," Danson wrote, "our house looked like a boarding house. Jess cooked, Ted and I shoveled snow. . . . On the 21st Jess fed eight for lunch." On Christmas Eve, the Dansons invited stranded scientists for dinner. One of the eighteen guests played his bagpipes, and Danson reported that, in spite of the weather, " . . . we had a fine Christmas Eve."

And though their children had left Flagstaff, other family members came to take their place. Jeffrey Lungé retired in 1968. No longer tied to California, the Lungés moved to Flagstaff onto the Research Center grounds. Ned lent the Homestead's garage to Jeffrey to use as a studio. Lungé, who had only occasionally painted Southwest themes up to that point, spent his days painting and touring the Colorado Plateau with Danson.

That summer, Jessica noticed that the Northland Press Building near the Museum had room for an art show. Ned Danson met with the Press's owner, suggesting that Lungé be given a chance to show his work. In 1968, the gallery held Jeffrey Lungé's first one-man show. A handful of the works were ocean scenes. The rest were of the Southwest. And every painting sold, a tradition that would last for Lungé's more than twenty-year-long career in Arizona. "One of the most exciting days of our life," Jessica wrote of the opening. "Everyone so responsive." The success of that show drew interest from gallery owners in Phoenix, and soon Lungé's paintings were being bought by such families as the Goldwaters and the Babbitts and such institutions as the Bank of Arizona, the Valley National Bank and museums from Santa Fe to Palm Springs. Danson purchased many of Jeffrey's paintings himself, some for his family and others for the Museum.

Lungé's paintings portrayed the beauty of the Arizona landscape that Ned Danson had loved from that first morning he had seen it. As the 1970s began, with the rise of the environmental movement, many people felt that this land was at risk. In Northern Arizona, these concerns rose along with the waters of Lake Powell behind Glen Canyon Dam. At about the same time, questions were raised by Vincent Schaefer, who had long worked on air pollution issues, about the effects of a proposed coal-burning power generation station on the air and water quality of the Colorado Plateau.

The Peabody Coal Company was already mining coal on the Navajo and Hopi reservations and pumping water from the

Eileen and Jeffrey Lungé at the opening of one of his one-man shows at the Main Trail Gallery, Scottsdale, Arizona

Ned Danson at opening of a Lungé show

Dan Perin, Duane Miller and Ned Danson at a Lungé show

Diane Miller, Judy Jansen and Pam Lungé (Jeffrey and Eileen's daughter) at a Lungé show opening night

aquifer serving both reservations, mixing it with the coal to send as a slurry though a pipeline to a generating station in Nevada. This company was preparing to mine more coal to service a second generating station near Page, Arizona. Environmental groups opposed their plans as did many Navajos and Hopis, who became concerned about the long-term effects of withdrawing massive amounts of water from their main aquifer. More science needed to be done. And the science already being done was not coordinated, leading to duplication of efforts, gaps in research and arguments about the implications of what was already known.

Conservationists and mining and power companies tended to present their arguments against and for the new power plant in absolutes. In order to present a more balanced, scientific perspective for the public, Barton Wright prepared a special exhibit at the Museum in 1970 called *Dams and Dilemmas*.

That same year, Danson sent out more than one hundred invitations to state and federal government agencies, businesses (including companies running the generating stations), academic institutions, conservation groups, and the Hopi and Navajo tribes, inviting them to attend a meeting in Page. Fifty-eight organizations sent representatives to the meeting, coming together to form CPEAC, the Colorado Plateau Environmental Advisory Council. They set as CPEAC's goals: coordination and promotion of research on the Colorado Plateau and sharing of findings among all members.

With funding provided primarily by the Navajo Generating Station, the Museum of Northern Arizona, and, due to Vincent Schaffer's influence, the State University of New York, Albany, CPEAC members worked together to publicize, through a newsletter, the environmental research that had been done, was being done, and still needed to be done on the Colorado Plateau. Beyond sharing information, CPEAC established a committee to evaluate research proposals based on their scientific merit. CPEAC itself funded some of the proposals and recommended funding of others by outside agencies. At CPEAC's next meeting at the Museum of Northern Arizona, Danson was elected chairman of the council as a whole, and a member of the Executive Committee. The Museum created a new Department of Environmental Studies to coordinate CPEAC's work and to administer other environmental research projects. Danson saw this as a continuation of Museum tradition. "Although it wasn't called environment in those days," Danson said, "we've been doing the basic research for many years."

That Christmas, Jan and Ted, their spouses—Ted having married his first wife, Randy Gosch, that year—and Ted's in-laws gathered with the Dansons, Jessica's mother and the Lungés at the Homestead for Christmas. Christmas Eve, the family participated in another Danson family tradition. "Everyone," Jessica wrote, "went out to cut down the Christmas tree and have a picnic in the snow. . . . Had a beautiful evening—twelve around the table for turkey—again in firelight and candlelight."

Dansons, Lungés, Goschs and Lucile MacMaster celebrate Christmas in the Homestead dining room, 1970

Christmas morning, everyone enjoyed exchanging large stockings, filled with all sorts of gifts from candy, books, and jewelry, to toothbrushes and toothpaste. "All twelve of us," Jessica wrote, "had a joyous time opening our stocking around the fireplace. Coffee and sweet rolls. Church at 11:00. Heavenly brunch. Some went to the Museum. The usual casual, happy Christmas night of drinks, fire, turkey sandwiches and charades (the game)."

After Christmas, the extended family traveled to Jan and Loren's home in La Jolla, California, to celebrate New Year's. On December 29, 1970, Jan woke her parents at their motel to tell them that Dr. Colton, who had been ill for nearly a year, had died.

Ned and Jessica returned to Flagstaff for a New Year's Day celebration of the life of Dr. Harold S. Colton at the Museum of Northern Arizona. Jessica wrote about it in a letter to her sisters-in-law:

Dr. Colton, that great gentleman and scholar, departed this life as quietly and humbly as he lived it, but what an impact he had on the lives of so many. . . . Because he had never been in the Church, Ned and I and Ferrell thought the most appropriate thing that could be done was to have the Museum open for friends to come and pay their respect. His closed coffin was [there] in the lobby, before the window, and the San Francisco Peaks stood out in all their glory that [afternoon]. The two huge Indian pots in the window were filled with greens and white chrysanthemums, and [there] were two huge gorgeous Navajo rugs on the floor. All the books had been taken off the racks at the desk, and just Dr. Colton's publications were out. They covered the entire rack, which was such a wonderful but quiet way of displaying his lifelong accomplishments. Members of the staff and of the Board of Trustees took turns being there during the hours of 1:00 to 5:00. At five the pallbearers quietly carried his coffin out. . . . We had all the family for dinner afterwards.

On her calendar, Jessica wrote, "One of the greats has left us."

A week after Dr. Colton died, his sister from Philadelphia wrote to Danson, "You have been so close to Harold all these years, that I really feel that I should write you a note of sympathy as though you were a real member of the family, for I know how much he thought of you and depended on you."

Years later, Ned wrote of Colton, "I miss him still."

After Colton's death, many things changed. The Museum lost a source of wisdom and experience, and one of its primary benefactors. Ned Danson became the Museum's elder statesman.

The Board of Trustees decided to hire an assistant director, Dr. William Lipe, the first since Danson had held the position, to share the burden of administration that Danson had borne on his own for years. Plans were made for the Dansons to move into the Coltons' home, now called Colton House, so that Lipe and his family could live in the Homestead.

But Colton House was not the only new home for the Dansons. As Jessica grew older, all the entertaining made her high blood-pressure worse, especially at Flagstaff's altitude of 7,000 feet. In 1969, the Lungé's bought a house in the community of Sedona, thirty miles south of the Museum, and Jessica, to get away, started visiting her sister. Sedona was, in those days, a small town. Its striking red-rock cliffs and mesas made it a popular site for filming Westerns, but had not yet attracted more than 2,700 residents. One day in the spring of 1971, Danson wrote, "Jessica and Eileen were walking down the little dirt lane [that ran past the Lungé's home] and came to a house with a sign 'House for Sale.' They spoke to me about it that weekend." After looking at the house and its beautiful gardens, orchard, and Oak Creek frontage, the Dansons fell in love. To have a weekend retreat close to the Lungés but away from Museum responsi-

Dr. William Lipe, the Museum's new assistant director, with Ned Danson, 1972

Colton House

Singing Waters, Sedona, 1971

bility was irresistible. They bought the house, named "Singing Waters," within the week.

That fall, the Dansons traveled to England and Scotland with the Lungés. In addition to touring the countryside and visiting British museums, Danson spent six weeks teaching Museum Studies and Archaeology of the Southwest at Leicester University. In the damp English weather, Danson developed a serious sinus infection and suffered an allergic reaction to the medication he was given. Ned and Jessica returned to Flagstaff in January of 1972. "It was good to be back at the Museum and to take up the old life again," Danson wrote, "There was only one problem and that was that my health wasn't as good as it should have been."

For the first time, Danson failed to publish his annual report on the Museum's activities in 1971, "due to the illness of the Director and an increase in administrative duties." Danson increasingly depended on the Museum's administrative staff, without which, Danson said "the Museum and Research Center would stagger to a halt. . . ." In his 1972 Annual Report,

Danson offered his compliments to "the comptroller's office, my secretary and the secretarial staff at the Research Center and at the Museum, for their hard work."

After the trip to Britain, Jessica began spending even more time in Sedona. While there, she attended Sunday services at the Chapel of the Holy Cross nestled in the Sedona red rocks. Mass at the Chapel was celebrated by the leader of the Spiritual Life Institute, a community of Roman Catholic monks in the Carmelite tradition. They were an experimental order, approved by Pope John XXIII. Informally calling themselves the "Nadans," they lived on an old ranch in the Village of Oak Creek, a few miles south of Sedona. The community of men and women lived in a single monastery, spending much of their time in solitude in their individual hermitages and the rest, working and praying together. Jessica found their contemplative Christianity invigorating and became an eager friend and supporter of the monks. Initially, Ned Danson was not as drawn to the Nadans as his wife was. Through his entire life, he looked to religion primarily to provide a sense of community and promote ethics. He was not a mystic. But he went with his wife to meet her new friends. "At first I resisted this," Danson wrote, "but as I got to know them I changed my thinking—changed it completely." Ned began to accompany Jessica to Mass when they spent the weekend in Sedona.

With renovations to Colton House completed in the spring of 1972, the Dansons moved into their new Flagstaff home. Ned loved it.

> Colton House was a delightful place to live. . . . The drive led up to a large stone house with a slate roof. One entered the living room through a short entrance hall. The room was most gracious. It was about 35 feet long and 20 feet wide. In the north wall was a long recessed window seat with windows looking out at the San Francisco Peaks. At the eastern end of the room was a large

Colton House living room, early 1970s

Colton House den, early 1970s

walk in fireplace with a . . . seat on both sides. . . . It was a charming house and a joy to live in. All the main bedrooms, the dining room and living room had fireplaces. . . . The house was snug, but I was glad I didn't have to pay for fuel.

Although a sturdier building and more beautiful than the Homestead, Colton House's large size proved to be a detriment for Jessica. The Dansons were now able to entertain more guests for lunch, tea, drinks and dinner—hosting five hundred in their first year. And as Colton House had a separate apartment, they also had many overnight guests—visiting scientists, family and friends—further draining Jessica.

When guests were present, Jessica missed her times of solitude in the tiny chapel she had created in Colton House. Without her quiet time, she felt her life was out of balance. Yet, she enjoyed the people she entertained, and always gracious, willingly shared her new home with guests, even when her husband was away. Ned Danson remembered one instance shortly after he and his wife moved into Colton House:

I had to go on a trip . . . and on my return . . . on a cold night I walked into the living room to find Jess sitting on the couch in front of the fire and standing nearby was Ferrell Colton. Each had a drink in their hands and as I entered the room—both toasted me and tossed their glass into the big wonderful fire place. Not to be left out—I took up a glass, filled it—drank it down and tossed mine into the fire—I think it surprised them for my glass was a crystal one and theirs a dime store, and I surprised myself.

The Dansons became grandparents in January, 1973, when their daughter gave birth to a boy, Eric, named for Jessica's father. Among the "pink ladies" working at the hospital that week was

Ned Danson sharing his love of cars with grandson Eric Penner Haury, 1973

Jan, Eric, Hulda and Emil Haury with Ned Danson decorating the Christmas tree in the Colton House dining room, 1973

Margaret "Chickie" Cooper, who had become close to the Dansons in the 1950s when she had worked at Kenyon Ranch, and later, had been Jan and Loren's neighbor in La Jolla the first year after they were married. Cooper, who became Eric's godmother, recognized Jan's name as she was doing her duties, and went to greet the new mother and her baby the day after he was born.

The Dansons arrived in La Jolla two days after the birth to meet their grandson and help care for him for a few weeks. That year, they made frequent trips to California to see their grandson, and Eric made his first trip to Arizona at Easter and spent his first Christmas at Colton House with his great-grandmother, both sets of grandparents, his parents and the Lungés. Even after the Haurys moved to Massachusetts, in 1974, so Loren could work at the Woods Hole Institution of Oceanography, the Dansons continued to see their grandson when board meetings took them to the East.

At Colton House, the Dansons continued to build friendships and integrate those friends into the life of the Museum. They became close to Dr. Walter and Nancy Taylor and their children, who lived nearby in Ferrell Colton's old home. The families met often. Jessica enjoyed inviting the children for tea at Colton House and letting them borrow children's books from their library. And through a series of meetings in Danson's new office next to Colton House, Ned and Nancy Taylor discussed creation of a group that would help bring the Museum and the greater Flagstaff community closer together.

This group was called "The Friends of the Museum." Danson described them in his annual report as a group of ten couples, led by Nancy Taylor, who "were interested in the Museum and in seeing it be of ever greater use to the schools and the community. . . . They are trying to develop programs to get the schools more involved in the Museum, and are lending a helping hand in many aspects of the Museum." The Friends offered a series of lectures for adults at the Museum, developed educational programs for fifth graders and provided hospitality at Museum

*Ned Danson, Frank Masland and Emil Haury in Spruce Tree House, Mesa Verde
National Park, during National Park Advisory Board and Council trip, 1971*

Ned Danson with Molly and Ray Thompson in Tucson, 1976

functions. "We welcome them, for they are the nuclei of a group that is going to be of ever greater help in the institution."

Danson also maintained his old friendships. His relationship with Senator Barry Goldwater, which had begun during his early years at the Museum, had grown stronger as time passed. The two men could rely on each other. A collector of Indian art from his youth, when Goldwater needed anything in his collection (or things he was considering adding to it) appraised, he would send it to the Museum, where the appraisal was done without charge. When the Senator wanted to donate any of his collection, Danson made sure the Museum was remembered. He did not always succeed. Despite Danson's efforts, the Heard Museum in Phoenix ended up acquiring the sizable Goldwater Katsina Doll Collection. But, in consolation, the Museum was able to acquire ten Navajo sandpaintings from his friend. And, through the years, Goldwater gave other works to the Museum.

Whenever Ned Danson went to Washington, he tried to stop in to see Senator Goldwater. And between visits, the two wrote to one another. The Museum's director often offered the Senator his opinion on legislation dealing with his field of expertise—such as overdevelopment of the Southwestern desert, about which Danson wrote "it is . . . [an] outrage the way they have cut up the country and sold poor little foolish people elsewhere land that is not fit to live on"—or matters of general interest such as the Vietnam War. In one letter, Danson mentioned that he "just came back from voting for you" before getting down to the real purpose of his letter.

And they discussed other things as two old friends would. In one set of correspondence, noting that mutual acquaintances had often said that the two men looked similar, Goldwater wrote to Danson, "I would hate to see you stuck with the reputation of looking like me. So one of us should grow a mustache."

But Danson disagreed. "Frankly I think we are two fine figures. And if I don't think you should grow a mustache and I don't want to, let's just go on as we are."

Danson's travel, both for business and family matters, did more than go on as it was. It increased. In addition to the regular collecting trips to the reservations, he began visiting his sisters in Ohio and New York more often, and both Dansons visited Jessica's widowed mother who was living in a retirement community in Claremont, California. They attended the opening performance of Ted's first Broadway play, *Status Quo Vadis*, a fortuitous choice for them, as it closed after the first night.

But even with the increased travel, Danson continued to fulfill his varied responsibilities. He remained chair of CPEAC and served on an increasing number of state and local boards, as well as serving as Chairman of the Southwest Parks and Monuments Association Board in 1973. At the Museum, he oversaw expansion of the library at the Research Center—renamed the Harold Sellers Colton Memorial Library—which tripled available library space. This growth required that the Museum install a sewer system. But the Museum could not be connected to the municipal sewers because it was outside Flagstaff's city limits. So Danson spent considerable time and effort, working with Flagstaff, to arrange for annexation of the Museum's property, allowing the sewer system to be installed. In spite of the effort, Danson wrote, "The alleviation of septic tanks and concomitant pollution problems more than make up for the trouble and disruption caused by the construction of the line."

In addition to adding to the library, Ned Danson expanded the Museum's publications. In 1973, he resumed publication of "Museum Notes," a newsletter for MNA members, focusing on people and events at the Museum. This complemented *Plateau*, the Museum's quarterly magazine, which published more scientific articles. The Museum's goal of publishing research findings continued with the periodic release of special technical bulletins on a variety of subjects. Meanwhile, several members of the staff wrote important books on botany, katsina dolls and Hopi silver.

Around that time, the director welcomed the American Association of Museums on-site Visiting Committee to MNA.

Ned Danson watching Barton Wright, MNA curator, sign one of Wright's books

This association had begun a new program to provide a "seal of approval that brings recognition to a museum for its commitment to excellence, accountability, high professional standards, and continued institutional improvement." Danson wrote in his 1973 Annual Report, "The Museum has received notification that it has passed the study and is now accredited . . . one of 278 museums accredited of over 500 applications." Both Danson and Barton Wright were invited to serve on teams, visiting other museums to evaluate them for accreditation.

By the mid-1970s, Danson recognized that opportunities for museums to acquire salvage archaeology contracts, a key source of revenue at the Museum, were diminishing. Although the Anthropology Department "accounted for the majority of outside research contracts and grants received by [the Museum]," Danson saw that, "in recent years the emphasis has shifted from salvage operations to that of conserving cultural and environmental resources." Companies realized that it was less expensive to reroute construction away from sites than to have them excavated. "Salvage archaeology is coming to be treated as a last resort . . . ," he observed. "We consider this a healthy trend, because it leads to the conservation of our ever-shrinking archaeological resource base." He added that "The Museum's Anthropology Department is certainly one of the national leaders in the development of methods for better survey and assessment of archaeological resources." However, the success the Museum had achieved in this area fostered competition. "Further evidence of our prominence in this field," Danson said, "is the fact that our junior archaeologists are frequently receiving lucrative job offers" from an increasing number of new private archeological and environmental consulting firms. As anthropologists left the Museum for private sector jobs, their grants went with them.

Although all the departments continued to grow, Museum funding no longer kept pace. The decline in resources affected the mood at the Museum. Lex Lindsay, head of the Museum's Anthropology Department, wrote that, "By the mid-seventies, your four busy curators were competing for resources for their dynamic programs, often squabbling with one another. At an infamous staff meeting you asked for some civility, or we would adjourn. We ignored you and you said this was the last staff meeting and so it was."

In November, 1974, CPEAC was dissolved, in part for lack of funding. The Navajo Generating Station was reluctant to renew its financial support, and Danson reported in May, 1974, that "MNA is presently operating on a deficit and cannot finance a scientist to head up an environmental studies department and CPEAC." "The Environmental Protection Agency, the Governor's Commission on the Environment, as well as the business community," Danson reported, "have all to a large degree learned to appreciate the need for being deeply involved in research to insure environmental concern." The Museum integrated CPEAC's library into its own. Danson wrote that "The library of CPEAC is invaluable, and by transferring it to the Museum's overall system, its contents are available for continued use."

Although CPEAC had ended, Danson's work with outside groups had not. He was appointed to the Arizona Water Resources Commission and continued to serve on the Southwest Parks and Monuments Association board. During his time on the National Park Service Advisory Council he was instrumental in gaining National Historic Landmark recognition for his old hometown of Glendale, Ohio, for being one of the first planned communities in the United States. Going beyond the job of advising which sites should become national parks or monuments, Danson also brought to the National Park Service his understanding of how to run museums. "On a trip to National Park Headquarters in Washington," he wrote, "I had found out that there was no person in overall charge of Park Service collections—their cataloguing and their care. It was appalling . . . that the Park Service had never had a system of controlling the millions of artifacts in the hundreds of areas of the Service. . . ." Danson persuaded the Park Service of the need for an official charged with overseeing the care of their extensive collections. The first person to hold that position, Ann Hitchcock, was a former MNA staff member.

During this time of intense work and regular travel, Danson's health started to decline. Decades of smoking had given him emphysema and heart problems. And his memory was fading. He could easily use his charm and social skills to cover up his growing forgetfulness, but details were starting to slip.

In 1974, Danson and the Board of Trustees determined that it was time for him to retire as director of the Museum. The board chose Dr. Hermann Bleibtreu, an anthropology professor at the University of Arizona and Dean of the Liberal Arts College, as Danson's successor. Bleibtreu was familiar with the Museum, as he had worked out of the Research Center on an archaeological dig during Danson's first summer as assistant director.

Danson was named President of the Museum's Board of Trustees, which let him continue to use his skills and contacts to help the Museum without having to deal with the day-to-day administrative details. In the July-August 1975 issue of "Museum Notes," Danson wrote:

> I am maintaining an office at the Annex, Dr. Colton's old office, where my time will be spent in working with the Board . . . on committees, in working on policy problems, in raising money . . . as well as preparing a new set of By-Laws to be ready for the 50th Anniversary of [the Museum].
>
> I intend to continue my activities with the Collector's Club, my interest in art, and in the environmental problems of Northern Arizona with which the Museum and I have long been concerned.

During his nineteen years at the Museum, Danson had worked to fulfill the original goals of the institution, even as it changed. He summarized that change in his last report to the

Board of Trustees. In 1956, MNA had a full-time staff of twelve plus eighteen part-time staff, visiting researchers and students. In 1974, Danson's last full year at the Museum, MNA had eighty-three full-time employees and ninety part-time staff, plus a large number of student and visiting researchers. The number of visitors to the Museum had expanded from less than 20,000 a year to over 100,000. The budget had grown twenty-five times, and Danson had overseen construction of three major additions at the Museum and another three at the Research Center. Many of the young scientists who had their professional start at the Museum in the late 1950s were now leading professors, researchers and artists across the country.

Danson's long-time friend Ray Thompson, Emil Haury's successor as Head of the University of Arizona's Department of Anthropology and Director of the Arizona State Museum, summarized Ned Danson's career:

> Ned had a quiet but effective style of leadership that guided the Museum from a family-funded organization to a modern institution at a time when many such organizations were failing to make that transition. He broadened the funding base, modernized the governance, attracted new donors, added to the collections, expanded research, enhanced public programs, and created opportunities for students, preparing MNA well for the changes of the late 20th century.

Ned Danson holding the Hopi plaque given to him at his retirement party, 1974

CHAPTER FIVE

AT HOME IN THE RED ROCKS
Retirement
1975- 2000

In preparation for Danson's retirement, Ned and Jessica made plans to move to Sedona full time. To make their small weekend cottage into a year-round house, he designed an extra wing for Singing Waters. A few months before Bleibtreu arrived to take over as director, with the Sedona house not yet finished, they moved out of Colton House so it could be made ready for his successor. The Dansons lived in an apartment on the Research Center grounds, built while Danson was the assistant director, until mid-July 1975, when the addition to Singing Waters was completed.

Sedona suited them well. Eileen and Jeffrey Lungé lived just a few minutes walk away. Ned and Jessica could drive to their friends the Nadans, in fifteen minutes, for Mass or company. A trip to the Museum to work, see old friends, or attend one of the Museum's board meetings or annual craftsman shows took little more than an hour.

The Dansons' creek-side home became a living reliquary of their lives. Ned, with his sense of style and experience with Museum displays, took the lead in organizing the interior of their home to make it as stunning as the red rock mesas visible from the windows. Navajo rugs covered their floors; old Navajo belts and Inca textiles shared space on the walls with *santos* from New Mexico. A collection of Jeffrey Lungé's Southwest paintings hung throughout the house, along with works by other Western artists like Maynard Dixon, Mac Schweitzer, and one of fall aspen trees by Mary-Russell Ferrell Colton, which she had given to Jessica many years earlier. Hopi katsina dolls and Pueblo pottery rested on shelves near works Ned had purchased while traveling on the *Yankee* and on his trip to Japan. Hand-carved furniture by Miss Yale, whom Ned Danson had met in North Carolina as a boy, was arranged throughout the house. The addition to the house included a small chapel for Jessica, decorated with a cherished carved crucifix and the *obi* that Danson had bought in Japan.

Their land had a small apple orchard, a field for growing vegetables, and a rose garden and lawn, watered by an irrigation ditch nearly as old as the Flagstaff Homestead. Danson added an English garden, which he loved to care for, just as his mother had cared for hers when he was a boy. He wrote to his daughter, "I have just come in from the rose garden where I've cut off all of the dead ones. . . . Then I went around and picked delphinium, columbine, blue campanula, coreopsis daisies and roses to make our bouquet for the morning. . . . When the grass was cut last week we looked like the best of English gardens."

Retirement, however, did not stop Ned Danson's work for the Museum or for Southwestern anthropology. He served as President of the Museum's Board of Trustees for five years, commuting several days a week the first year to his old office next to Colton House.

Danson then took an office in Sedona's newly built Tlaquepaque shopping area on Oak Creek, only half a mile upstream from his home. Tlaquepaque was modeled after the city and historic folk art center of the same name near Guadalajara, Mexico. The colonial Mexican-style buildings, purposefully designed so as not to cut down any of the many sycamore trees that had been growing in the area before development, appealed to Danson's sense of history and natural beauty. When in town, he went to his new office nearly ever weekday. When people came to visit him there, he made sure to take them to the nearby shops, a

Ned Danson tending roses in his Sedona garden

fact one of the store owners, Ann Fabricant, expressed gratitude for years later.

> I first met Ned in 1977 when I opened my shop at Tlaquepaque. . . . Ned would stop in on his way to his office, offering kind words and good cheer. He always brought his guests and business associates in the store and strongly suggested that they buy something. . . . [Knowing] a person of his integrity and caliber buoyed me up. . . . Later when we began the Native American Invitational Art Show, he so willingly offered his support and with his reputation gave us the credibility we sought. With Ned as a judge, we were able to attract other judges of good credentials and Native American artists wanted to participate in a show that he would be part of. To win an award from him meant a great deal.

Danson continued to be active as a member of several national and state organizations. He remained a member of the National Park Service Advisory Council until its demise in the early 1980s. His service on the Southwest Parks and Monuments Association Board continued until 1986. When he left SPMA–later renamed the Western National Parks Association (WNPA)—the organization recognized him by establishing the Edward B. Danson Distinguished Associate Award. The Danson Award is given to selected WNPA employees "for contributions to greater public understanding of the importance of the National Parks." Around the same time, he left the board of the Arizona Historical Society, created in 1864 to collect and preserve "all facts relating to the history of the Territory" of Arizona.

In 1976, Danson was appointed by the Speaker of the United States House of Representatives to the board of trustees of the American Folklife Center of the Library of Congress, a new board tasked with preserving and promoting American folklife—from arts and crafts to music, drama, and ritual. Danson became its president in 1980. Alan A. Jabbour, Director of the American Folklife Center, praised Danson's experience. "Ned was a great board member, and for a period a great chairman. He brought to bear on his board service an amazing blend of strong leadership and sensitive support. I think he made deep and important contributions to the development and direction of the American Folklife Center. And he certainly gave me great guidance as a young director."

As enjoyable as Danson found his trips to the nation's capitol, he still relished his adventures into Arizona's high desert country. And he made them often. A month after one of the American Folklife Center's Board meetings in 1977, he visited Canyon de Chelly and Keams Canyon, and took his second river trip through the Grand Canyon with his old friend, meteorologist and Museum board member, Vincent Schaefer.

Sometimes, the people Danson encountered on his Arizona excursions surprised him. He recalled one encounter in the late

1970s when he was driving through Indian Country, going, as he admitted, "about 85 . . . when I saw a police van. . . . I pulled out and stopped before he got to me and was standing by the [Mercedes] with my driver's license out."

But as the officer prepared to write a ticket, Danson recognized a familiar name on his brass nametag. It was the same name as a prominent artist he had come to know during his years at the Museum. He asked the officer if he was a relative.

"He looked up, and said, 'yes' and I said and meant it—'She is a great woman and a fine leader.'"

The officer "smiled and said, 'I'm just making out a warning ticket,' which he gave me. We chatted a moment and then I drove on. . . ."

Ned and Jessica often visited Tucson to see Emil and Hulda Haury and welcomed them many times to Singing Waters. Later in the same year when he went down the Colorado River with Schaefer, Danson accompanied Haury on a field trip to a Paleo-Indian site on the Lehner Ranch, where Haury had earlier excavated the bones of nine mammoths, a horse, a bison and a tapir in association with hearths and Clovis spear points more than 10,000 years old.

For several years after retiring, Danson continued one of his favorite activities: going on collecting trips for the Museum's Hopi Show.

Barton [Wright], Willie Coin and I drove out to make the annual collection of Hopi material for the . . . Hopi Show. I spent two days going from house to house asking the ladies if they had anything to send in for the exhibition for judging and for sale. . . .

Many would say come in—sit down—and then bring out a basket, a sash or robe, a pot, etc. They would tell us what they wanted for the pot and then we would examine it—no cracked pots—no aniline dyes in baskets—no cotton warps on rugs—etc.

Ned Danson and Vincent Schaefer on river trip through the Grand Canyon, 1977

Ned Danson and Emil Haury at Singing Waters

Ned Danson and Elizabeth White (Polingaysi Qoyawayma) during the 1980 tribute to Danson at the Museum of Northern Arizona

Ned Danson and Emil Haury cooking Wetherill Stew in dutch ovens during field trip to the mammoth kill site on the Lehner Ranch, 1977

After his retirement, relationships Danson had built with Hopi elders remained strong. He later recalled:

> It was in 1976, during the summer, that five Hopi elders came to see me in my office. They asked if I would go with them on a trip to show me the markers for the Hopi boundaries. They want this done so that a respected *Bahana* (white man) would be able to say in court that I had been shown the boundaries of the Hopi land—not the reservation, but the land the Hopi claimed as their native use area. I agreed to go with them.

Ned Danson remained President of the Museum of Northern Arizona's Board of Trustees until the end of 1979 and would remain a member of the board through 1985. On his leaving the presidency, the Museum celebrated Danson's twenty-seven years of service with an exhibit of art and crafts, purchased at the Museum while he was director and, later, president of the board. As part of the celebration, Emil Haury organized an evening "Tribute to Ned Danson," which included a gift of a bust of Ned done by Sedona artist and neighbor, Bob Kittredge.

Danson moved his office from Tlaquepaque to a remodeled workshop at his Sedona home. There, he continued to prepare for meetings of the boards on which he still served and to write to family, friends and colleagues. He also worked with other residents of Sedona to try to protect from development a large area of the red rock cliffs and canyons around Sedona, by making it part of the National Park Service.

"There was, of course, a large uproar that this would deprive 'the people' of their land," Danson recalled. It was an allegation he denied. He wrote government officials, including Arizona Governor Bruce Babbitt, a scion of one of the Flagstaff ranching families Danson had known so well, and a former researcher at the Museum. A friend and close Danson ally on this matter, Representative Morris Udall, gave a speech on the issue on the floor of the House of Representatives.

"The loss of this scenic area," Danson said, "will be a loss for all of America."

But unlike with so many of his efforts, Danson failed to achieve his goal of creating a national park in the red rock country north of Sedona.

Despite that setback, he continued working. He joined with Keep Sedona Beautiful in efforts to set aside some of the land as a national wilderness area, and in the 1980s three wilderness areas were created near Sedona.

Ned and Jessica also contributed to their new community by participating in its cultural scene. They supported chamber music in Sedona and, with the Lungés, the Sedona Art Center. Danson also became president of his neighborhood improvement association and used his administrative skills to untangle the complexities of the neighborhood's water rights, clarifying not only his own family's claims but those of his neighbors.

With the Lungés living just a few doors away for most of Danson's retirement, he always had family nearby. And over the course of the 1970s, more family moved within driving distance. After almost five years at Woods Hole Oceanographic Institution in Massachusetts, Loren Haury received a job offer from the Scripps Institution of Oceanography in San Diego, California, and the family moved to Del Mar in 1978. They made regular trips to Arizona, dividing time between the Haurys in Tucson and the Dansons in Sedona. Ted, married now to his second wife, Casey Coates, also moved to California. He had begun his TV and stage career in New York and received his first break in a recurring role as a lawyer on a soap opera called *Somerset*. In 1978, shortly after his move west, Ted spent the good part of one Thanksgiving visit to Sedona standing in the cold outside his parents' home, practicing the bagpipes for his role as the murder victim in the movie *The Onion Field*.

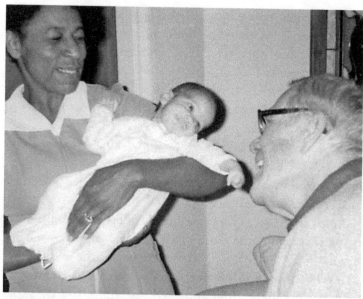

Ned Danson with granddaughter Kate Danson and nurse, 1980

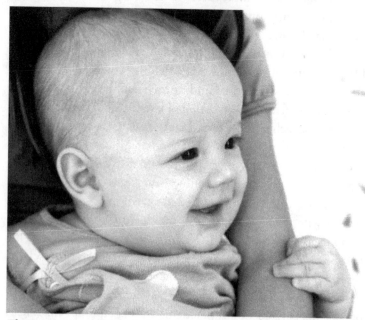

The Dansons' granddaughter Alexis "Kat" Danson, 1984

Danson family gathering in 1984. (Left to right, back row) Jan Haury, Casey, Ned, Kate and Jessica Danson; (front row) Ted and Alexis "Kat" Danson, Eric and Loren Haury

In 1979, Ted became a father, his first daughter Kate being born on Christmas Eve, 1979, under tragic circumstances. Casey suffered a stroke while giving birth and underwent months of rehabilitation. Ned and Jessica, already having joined Ted and Casey before the birth, extended their stay to care for their infant granddaughter while Casey recovered. In 1985, Ted and Casey adopted a second daughter, originally named Alexis, a name she later changed to Katrina, or Kat.

The support Ned and Jessica had given Ted's dream of acting proved wildly successful when their son was cast in the role of Sam Malone on the TV sitcom *Cheers*, a role that catapulted him into international fame and eventually earned him two Emmy Awards in its eleven-year run. Ned Danson found the experience of having a famous son to be pleasant but odd. For years, because Dr. Danson had been the center of focus at the Museum, Ted had been "Ned Danson's son." Now, as Ned went through Sedona stores, he overheard people talking about him as "Ted Danson's father."

In most ways, however, Ted's success did not affect either of his parent's lives, although they attended the filming of *Cheers* and were extras in a film Ted made in Arizona in the mid-1990s. They did, however, enjoy sharing private jet flights in and out of Sedona through Ted's generosity.

The Dansons traveled regularly, by jet or by car, visiting family and friends in California and the East. They made several summer trips to Victoria, British Columbia, a place said by some to be more English than England, where the Lungés spent many of their summer months.

The Dansons also became closer to the Nadans, even as the monks themselves moved farther away. The Nadans found that development around their Sedona monastery made it difficult to maintain the solitude they craved. Reluctantly, they sold their Sedona chapel and hermitages and moved to Crestone, Colorado. There, the Dansons became regular visitors, and even funded construction of one of the guest hermitages, which they used during several month-long retreats.

This bond made Jessica feel closer to Roman Catholicism than to the Episcopal Church that she and Ned had been members of since birth. Even though Ned had served for several years on the Episcopal Church's vestry in Sedona, he felt less comfortable when a split developed at the church. The Dansons decided to convert to Roman Catholicism, making their vows at Nada Hermitage in Colorado.

Although Ned Danson was retired, his work was still recognized in Washington, D.C. In 1986, he was awarded the Department of Interior's Conservation Award "in recognition of his many significant contributions to research on, and preservation of, the natural and cultural resources of the Colorado Plateau. . . ." The ceremony was held in the Interior Department's Auditorium, with a joint honor guard and music by the Marine Band. This citation served as a capstone for his career. It listed his numerous accomplishments, observing that "Dr. Danson has furthered the activities of not only the National Park Service, but also the U.S. Geological Survey, the Bureau of Indian Affairs, and the Bureau of Land Management. . . ." The citation stated that he "was instrumental in the 1980's in increasing National Park Service attention to its vast museum collections, and recommended numerous actions that have subsequently been implemented to strengthen cultural resource management in the National Park Service." It also praised him for "his more than thirty years of deep commitment and efforts towards the preservation of natural and cultural resources. . . ."

In a letter, Danson thanked those who had written him after receiving the Interior Department honor. "When I think of the amount of history that we read and reviewed for the Park Service, and the areas studied for future possible parks and monuments, I realize it was a monumental study. . . . The National Parks and Monuments system is one of the great concepts in America. It seems to me that I have been deeply rewarded in being allowed to work with them."

The following year, Ned Danson suffered a heart attack, and his focus started to narrow. He spent more of his energy on local institutions—serving on the boards of Flagstaff's Lowell Observatory and the Northern Arizona Natural History Association and becoming a member of the Sedona Car Club, as well as continuing to attend Museum board meetings as an emeritus member.

But he did become a member of one board that required him to drive to Tucson, that of the Tohono Chul Park, a botanical garden founded by Dr. Colton's nephew, Dr. Richard Wilson, and his wife Jean. The park highlighted desert art and Native culture, as well as natural history.

He also became a founding member, in 1987, of the Board of Arizona Indian Living Treasures, an organization dedicated to honoring lifetime achievements of Arizona Native American artists and educators, which had been created by Ann Fabricant, the store owner he had befriended at Tlaquepaque. Another early member of the board, Hopi Emory Sekaquaptewa, later said that "Ned . . . helped us immensely in the critical first years of our development." He added, "His support and interest in the Hopi culture were instrumental in building the success of the Hopi Show at the Museum which in turn helped build recognition of many Hopi artists."

When Ned Danson's banker-nephew Dan Perin wished to move to Arizona from New York, he applied for work at the Bank of Arizona. Perin turned to his Uncle Ned, a friend of the bank's president. Danson vouched for the skills and character of the man who had once lied to him and then "killed" him in the Homestead bathroom during a game of Murder. "I think Uncle Ned made the difference," said Perin, who would become a member of the Museum's Board of Trustees and in 1991 would establish the Edward Bridge Danson, Jr., Endowed Chair in Anthropology at the Museum.

Dan's sister, Cynthia "Cindy" Perin, moved to Sedona in 1989, motivated by love of the land and of her uncle, who had introduced her to it. Following in the tradition of Danson's uncle, Bill Allen, and of Danson himself, they became the third generation of the family to move to Arizona. After her move, Cindy called Ned and Jessica every morning to see that they were all right. This call joined taking tea and reading Morning Prayer as a part of the Dansons' early morning ritual.

When the Dansons' next door neighbor decided to sell his home in 1986, Ted purchased it. Adjacent to the house and its orchard was a small field. The Dansons looked after the field for their son, and, when someone who had been farming a portion of the land asked if some Hopis he knew could use a fallow section, Ned readily agreed. Every year since, Hopi families have come to the field to plant corn and other crops. Especially during drought years, much of the corn used in Hopi ceremonies was grown in Ted's field. Even as Danson's health slowly declined, Hopi friends were, at times, only a few minutes' walk away.

Ned and Jessica Danson with nephew, Edward Bridge Danson "Dan" Perin (left) in the Dansons' Sedona home

Ned Danson and family gather in Cortez, Colorado, before San Juan River trip, 1990. (Left to right) Dan and Reuben Perin, Ned and Ted Danson, Loren Haury, Rick Muhlhauser

Ned Danson made one of his last visits to the Hopi Reservation in 1993 to introduce his grandson Eric to the land and people he loved. As they were guided by a Hopi along a village street, an old woman who recognized them from their Museum days rushed up as quickly as she could, crying "Dr. Danson! Dr. Danson!" and offered him some bread, which he gratefully accepted. On the trip, the family visited numerous Hopi friends. Among them was Vera, a woman who for years had made piki bread as a demonstrator during the Hopi Shows. "She jumped up out of her couch when we came in," Danson recalled, "her face lit up like a candle and she scurried over to get some piki bread, a roll for each one of us. She always gives us a present when we visit. . . . We found out from her son that she is 108 years old!"

By the 1990s, more and more friends Danson had known for years were dying. Emil Haury died in 1993, Jeffrey Lungé, one year later. At the beginning of the decade, Danson brought Ted, Loren and three of his nephews together for a trip down the San Juan River. It would be his last significant adventure into the wilderness of the Colorado Plateau. The trip was led by Bob Lister, a friend from Harvard, and the man Danson had succeeded at the University of Colorado in 1949. The group hiked to Moon House cliff dwelling, Lister's favorite archaeological site. While climbing up a rock ledge on the way back, Lister suffered a heart attack and fell. A doctor who had just visited Moon House, and was still in the area, declared that Lister had probably died before hitting the ground.

As Danson's heart grew weaker and his emphysema worse, his memory problems accelerated. In 1994, on Ned and Jessica's last trip to Britain to visit Ted, who was filming in Scotland, Danson sat down to write a letter to his old friend Jimmy Robinson. He told her that his hotel room had a wonderful view of Edinburgh Castle. But they were staying near Inverness. They had not even passed through Edinburgh on this trip. When Jessica read what he had written, she cried out, "Oh, Ned," in surprise and confusion. On that same trip, Danson fell down the steps outside the manor house where they were staying, and suffered a back injury that never fully healed, in spite of later spinal surgery.

Although that was his last foreign trip, Danson traveled east on several occasions to see his sisters. On one trip, Danson drove with his niece Cindy Perin to see her mother. The drive was eventful. With Cindy at the wheel of her Honda Civic, they had barely driven three miles before Danson declared, "I think we need to go back. I forgot my heart medicine!"

"So back we went," Cindy recalled. "You can imagine everyone's surprise when we drove back in the driveway not fifteen minutes later. . . . I knew we were in for a fun time."

They began the trip again, but at a stop in Gallup, Danson asked his niece if he could drive for a while.

I said "sure," not realizing that I was giving my life into the hands of a man who, I think, secretly wished he could have been a race car driver like Mario Andretti. We were about 2 hours from Albuquerque when I noticed a train in the distance and remarked how wild west that looked. Uncle Ned looked over and at that moment I looked ahead and there in front of us was a large blown tire just waiting to be hit. All I could calmly say was, "Oh, Uncle Ned." Not a word was said between the two of us. Uncle Ned swerved to try and miss the tire but hit it with the front left tire of the car, the car went sideways, trembled and all I could think was *not four hours from home and we are going to die!*

Suddenly the car stopped shaking, went straight and we continued on as if nothing had happened. No words were spoken for at least thirty seconds when Uncle Ned [turned] to me and said, "I did that pretty well, don't you think?"

Shortly after the incident, Cindy noticed that her car was shaking again and saw that the speedometer read eighty-five miles per hour.

Ned Danson celebrating his 81st birthday with Cynthia "Cindy" Perin in her Sedona home, 1997

"We slowed to seventy-five," she said, "but not long after, eighty-five was again topped. We laughed and made it to Albuquerque for lunch but I stated that I thought I would drive for a while." A while lasted the remainder of the trip.

A couple years later, when she spoke to him about the trip, he said, "Oh yeah, that was nice," not showing any indication of remembering the tire, the speeding, or the lost medicine. But he did add, "You never let me drive again after Albuquerque!"

After his sisters' deaths, Danson's trips east became rare. His last was to Martha's Vineyard for Ted's marriage to Mary Steenburgen, a wedding attended by Mary's friend, then sitting President Bill Clinton, whom Danson had forgotten he'd voted for. Ned and Jessica were delighted to welcome their new daughter-in-law and quickly started counting Mary's children,

Mary Steenburgen and Ted Danson wedding, Martha's Vineyard, 1995. (Left to right) Lilly McDowell, Kate Danson, Charlie McDowell, Mary, Ted and Alexis "Kat" Danson

Gathering of the family at Singing Waters, late 1990s. (Left to right, back row) Loren, Ned, Lilly, Alexis, Jan, Jessica, Eileen Lungé and granddaughter Karis Miller; (front row) Charlie, Eric, Mary, Ted, Kate, and Mary's mother, Nell Steenburgen

Lilly and Charlie McDowell, as their grandchildren. The Dansons of Sedona enjoyed hosting the "Danburgens" of Los Angeles, as Ted introduced the new members of his expanded family to the land where he grew up.

Over the next few years, Ned Danson began to show other signs of old age. He began to require supplemental oxygen, rarely at first, but full time after breaking his ribs in a fall into Singing Waters' irrigation ditch. This led to his greatest loss, when, because of his injuries, he was convinced to stop driving his beloved Mercedes. His family had been arguing for years that he should stop driving, but he had refused. And for a while, after finally relenting, he seemed to forget his promise to give up driving a bit more often than he forgot other things.

But while his memory and his physical strength faded, his personality never did. He remained as engaging and social as ever. He could still tell tales from his youth, even though he had difficulty recalling what happened that day, and could charm his way through a conversation he could no longer fully follow.

In 1999, Loren Haury retired from Scripps Institution of Oceanography. He and Jan moved into the house Ted owned next to Singing Waters. The next year, their son Eric moved to Sedona as well, becoming the fourth generation of the family to live in the state Ned Danson loved.

A few months later, Ned, Jessica and Eileen Lungé were driven by Ted to a place where they could take a gentle walk through the red rocks. While the others walked, Danson stayed behind in the car. When they returned from their walk, they found him sitting in the driver's seat. Ted had driven them there and expected to drive back. But when Ned's and Ted's eyes met, Ted saw a silent pleading look in his father's eyes and couldn't bring himself to ask to take the wheel. Ned Danson was allowed to drive the family home.

It was his last drive.

A week later, on November 30, 2000, Jessica left Ned for a few minutes as he was watching one of his favorite television programs, *This Old House*. When she came back into the room, Ned Danson had died.

A few days later, he was cremated. His ashes were placed in a Hopi bean pot, which was sealed with a bowl made by one of Danson's favorite Hopi potters, Garnet Pavatea. As his funeral started at St. John Vianney Catholic Church, the people gathering to celebrate Danson's life embodied for one last time the merging of the many worlds Danson had inhabited.

Close kin still living in Cincinnati shared seats with a man who had traveled with Irving and Exy Johnson on one of their last *Yankee* voyages. Archaeologists who had studied under Danson at the University of Arizona sat near owners of shops Danson had patronized. Nadan monks spoke with Hopi elders. Jimmy Robinson, who had introduced Ned to his future bride, gathered with people who had known and worked with Danson at Point of Pines.

Many came from the Museum of Northern Arizona. They included former staff and students—some still working in the disciplines they had learned under Danson's leadership, others merely keeping the memories of those days alive.

Ned Danson was buried in the family plot that already held the remains of his brother-in-law, Jeffrey Lungé. As his ashes were laid into the red, iron-rich dirt, his niece Cindy began singing "Amazing Grace." And although it had not been planned, friends and family formed a line, and each tossed a handful of Sedona soil onto the pot containing Danson's ashes, silent except for the song. Ted completed the task of filling the hole.

Five years later, Jessica followed her husband in death, and many of the same people assembled for another funeral. Like Ned, Jessica was cremated, her ashes sealed in a small wooden box.

The day before the burial service, Jan and Loren Haury went to dig the new grave in the family plot. While Jan was taking her turn, she said that the soil she was digging suddenly felt softer. Loren's training as an anthropologist's son told him what that meant. The family had forgotten precisely where in the plot Ned

Danson has been buried, but the soft soil was a clear sign that they were excavating a burial.

Loren took the shovel and, like an archaeologist wary of causing damage, carefully removed layers of dirt, placing them in a pile near the grave. A minute or so later, the pot containing Ned Danson's ashes was visible once more. Just as Danson had uncovered the remains of others in the past, so his were uncovered now. His pot was left in place to be pointed out during Jessica's service the next day.

At the ceremony, the Dansons' grandchildren set the box containing Jessica's ashes in the grave next to her husband's remains. And the tradition that had started at Ned Danson's funeral was repeated.

The guests lined up before the pile of soil. Family, colleagues, and friends, handful by handful, scattered the dirt on both box and pot. Over the slow, silent minutes, Ned and Jessica, together forever, were covered up, and vanished, absorbed into the Arizona land that they loved.

Dr. Kelley Hays-Gilpin, the Danson Chair of Anthropology, Museum of Northern Arizona, 2010

AFTERWORD

The Edward Bridge Danson
Chair of Anthropology

A Bridge to the Future

In 1990, the Arizona State Museum in Tucson was preparing an exhibit on Hopi Yellow Ware pottery, past and present. The young anthropologist setting up the display was surprised to see an elderly man step over the ropes protecting her work area. He approached and began asking questions about what she was doing, as though he belonged there. When she asked who he was, he introduced himself as Ned Danson, former director of the Museum of Northern Arizona. She introduced herself as Kelley Hays. Neither of them knew then that one day she would sit in his chair in his old office at the Museum of Northern Arizona's Research Center as the first person to hold the Edward Bridge Danson, Jr., Endowed Chair in Anthropology.

The Danson Chair was created in 1991 by Ned Danson's nephew, Edward B. Danson "Dan" Perin, a member and officer of the Museum of Northern Arizona's Board of Trustees. The purpose of the Danson Chair endowment was to provide funding for an anthropologist who would "dedicate . . . majority time to research-related anthropological endeavors and as needed be engaged in exhibition, public program and collection management services on behalf of the Museum." The Chair honors the legacy created by the institution's founders, Harold S. and Mary-Russell Ferrell Colton, and maintained by Danson as he shepherded the Museum through years of dramatic growth.

In September, 2006, sixteen years after the Danson and Hays encounter in Tucson, Dr. Robert Breunig, Director of the Museum of Northern Arizona, appointed Dr. Kelley Hays-Gilpin, Associate Professor of Anthropology at Flagstaff's Northern Arizona University, (now a full professor) as the first person to hold the Danson Chair. "We feel incredibly honored to appoint Dr. Kelley Hays-Gilpin to the Danson Chair," Dr. Breunig said at the time of her appointment. "She is not only a first rank scholar of Southwestern anthropology; she embodies the spirit of graciousness and devotion to the mission of the Museum that was exemplified by Dr. Danson."

Hays-Gilpin, like Danson, studied anthropology at the University of Arizona, getting her Ph.D. there in 1992. Also like him, she had ties with the Museum for many years before joining its staff. She wrote her dissertation in one of the "chicken coops" at the Research Center in 1991 and became a Research Associate of the Museum in 1992.

After completing her doctorate, she worked for the Navajo Nation Archaeology Department for seven years, then was hired to teach anthropology classes at Northern Arizona University. Since then, she has done research and published on a number of topics, including prehistoric rock art, textiles, baskets, gender studies, and Hopi prehistoric pottery and iconography. Much of this work was done in collaboration with native tribes, especially the Navajo and Hopi.

Over the decades since Ned Danson first studied archaeology at the University of Arizona, anthropology has evolved. When Danson went on his first archaeological excavation in 1939, the focus was more on obtaining cultural treasures to display in museums. By the time he received a Ph.D. in 1952, anthropology had changed significantly. At the Museum of Northern Arizona, from its earliest days, Dr. and Mrs. Colton had worked closely with the Hopi and Navajo tribes. During Danson's tenure at the Museum, he continued the Coltons' approach. Since then, the partnership between scientists and Native peoples has deepened as tribal members have earned their own advanced degrees in anthropology. Anthropological research has grown from cooperation with tribal members to collaboration. As archaeologist Raymond Thompson, former director of the Arizona State Museum, Danson's friend and colleague and one of Hays-Gilpin's mentors, wrote:

> Great changes took place in archaeology and anthropology during Ned's lifetime. More changes are obviously on the horizon. We need to exploit the intellectual energy that comes from merging the knowledge of the native world with the time-tested techniques for studying the past that have been accumulated over the last couple hundred years. This can only be accomplished through the kind of fruitful collaboration with our native colleagues that Kelley is carrying out.

A major focus of Hays-Gilpin's work, since being named to the Danson Chair, has been the Hopi Iconography Project. The Museum of Northern Arizona has in its collection several murals fragments recovered from Awat'ovi, an ancestral Hopi pueblo, excavated in the 1930s by Danson's mentors Jo Brew and Watson Smith. Hays-Gilpin, in collaboration with members of the Hopi Tribe, compared the Awat'ovi murals with prehistoric and historic art from other pueblos of the Southwest and Mexico. Following the recommendations of her Hopi co-workers, "We're talking about what they mean," she wrote about the images, "and why they are important to people today." Working with Hopis Leigh Kuwanwisiwma, who heads the Hopi Cultural Preservation Office, artists Michael Kabotie and Delbridge Honanie, and others, Hays-Gilpin and rock art specialist Polly Schaafsma edited a book in 2010 on the subject, *Painting the Cosmos: Metaphor and Worldview in Images from the Southwest Pueblos and Mexico*. When co-author Kabotie, also a poet and jeweler, passed away unexpectedly in 2010, Hays-Gilpin helped prepare a special Museum exhibit of his work and vision.

Since being named to the Danson Chair, Hays-Gilpin has also overseen the Colton Ceramic Repository for Colorado Plateau pottery and edited publications on ceramics for the Museum's Ceramic Series. And she has worked with both the Hopi and Navajo on repatriation of cultural material from the Museum's collection back to the tribes.

In 2010, the Museum of Northern Arizona launched a fund-raising effort to complete the endowment of the Danson Chair. When Hays-Gilpin was hired, the endowment was partially funded, so during her first four years she was able to work only one day a week at the Museum. With additional funding, she plans to carry out several of the programs she and Breunig agreed were important for the Museum when she was first hired. "We want NAU students to feel at home at the Museum," she said in the Museum's newsletter announcing her appointment in the fall of 2006. "Students can engage in service learning while helping their community. [NAU is starting] to offer classes in museum studies and will establish a Native-American focused museum studies program." In addition, from its earliest days, important research on the Colorado Plateau has been done at the Museum by retired scientists. Hays-Gilpin recognizes that anthropologists will continue to retire to Flagstaff, in part because of the library, collections and staff at the Museum, and she wants to have the time and funds to coordinate their research with the Museum's other programs. Continuing the Museum's tradition of publishing research done on the Colorado Plateau, Hays-Gilpin also anticipates spending more time expanding the Museum's anthropological publications.

Ned Danson served the Museum as a bridge in the 1960s and 1970s—taking it from a private, family-financed and family-run museum and research institution of the Colton era to the larger, independent museum, collections and research center of the mid-1970s. Kelley Hays-Gilpin, as the first Danson Chair, continues that tradition, serving as a bridge into the 21st century. In all that

she does, she continues Ned Danson's passion for the mission of
the Museum as stated in its original constitution:

> To increase and diffuse knowledge and appreciation of
> science and art and maintain in the City of Flagstaff a
> Museum; to collect and preserve objects of art and sci-
> entific interest; to protect historic and prehistoric sites,
> works of art, scenic places, and wildlife from needless
> destruction; to provide facilities for research, and to of-
> fer opportunities for aesthetic enjoyment.

Jan Danson Haury

REFERENCES

BOOKS AND MONOGRAPHS

Colbert, Edwin H. 1989. *Digging into the Past: An Autobiography*. Dembner Books, New York.

Brugge, David M. 1993. *Hubbell Trading Post National Historic Site*. Southwest Parks and Monuments Association, Tucson.

Danson, Edward Bridge. 1957. *An Archaeological Survey of West Central New Mexico and East Central Arizona*. Papers of the Peabody Museum of Archaeology and Ethnology, Harvard University, 44(I), Cambridge.

Haury, Emil W. 1985. *Mogollon Culture in the Forestdale Valley East-central Arizona*. The University of Arizona Press, Tucson.

————. 1989. *Point of Pines, Arizona: A History of the University of Arizona Archaeological Field School*. The University of Arizona Press, Tucson.

Johnson, Captain and Mrs. Irving. 1936. *Westward Bound in the Schooner* Yankee. W. W. Norton and Company, New York.

Manchester, Albert and Ann Manchester. 1993. *Hubbell Trading Post National Historic Site: An Administrative History*. National Park Service Division of History, Southwest Cultural Resources Center, Professional Paper, No. 46, Santa Fe.

Mangum, Richard K. and Sherry G Mangum. 1997. *One Woman's West: The Life of Mary-Russell Ferrell Colton*. Northland Publishing, Flagstaff.

Miller, Jimmy H. 1991. *The Life of Harold Sellers Colton: A Philadelphia Brahmin in Flagstaff*. Navajo Community College Press, Tsaile, Arizona.

Olberding, Susan Deaver. 1997. *Telling the Story: The Museum of Northern Arizona*. Plateau, Museum of Northern Arizona, Flagstaff.

Reid, J. Jefferson and Stephanie M. Whittlesey. 2010. *Prehistory, Personality, and Place: Emil W. Haury and the Mogollon Controversy*. The University of Arizona Press, Tucson.

Root, Evelyn C. 1968. *The Museum of Northern Arizona*. K. C. Publications, Flagstaff.

Smith, Watson. 1969. *The Story of the Museum of Northern Arizona: An address before the Newcomen Society, September 21, 1968*. Museum of Northern Arizona, Flagstaff.

————. 1984. *One Man's Archaeology*. Tucson.

————. 1987. *Handy Guide for Doggerelists*. Edited by Benjamin Smith and Carol A. Gifford. The Morgue Publishing Company Resurrected, Tucson.

Unknown. 1980. *A Tribute to Ned Danson: May 3 through June 8*, Museum of Northern Arizona, Flagstaff, Arizona.

ARTICLES

Chase, Katherin. 1983. "Museum Receives Burr Collection." *Museum Notes,* Museum of Northern Arizona, New Series, 11(5):1.

Colton, Mary-Russell Ferrell. 1930. "The Hopi Craftsman." *Museum Notes,* Museum of Northern Arizona, 3(1):1-4.

Cosulich, Bernice. 1942. "Three Centuries of Tubac History." *Arizona Highways,* 18(10):14-19, 40-41.

Danson, Edward, and Harold E. Molde. 1950. "Casa Malpais, A Fortified Pueblo Site at Springerville." *Plateau,* Museum of Northern Arizona, 22(4):61-67.

Danson, Edward B. 1958. "The Glen Canyon Project." *Plateau,* Museum of Northern Arizona, 30(3):75-78.

————. 1971. "Testimony at Hearings Before the Committee on Interior and Insular Affairs, United States Senate 92nd Congress at Page, Arizona on May 28, 1971." Published in *Problems of Electrical Power Production in the Southwest.*

————. 1978. "The Museum of Northern Arizona: A Brief History." *Plateau,* Museum of Northern Arizona, Fiftieth Anniversary Issue, 50(4):4-7.

Haury, Emil W. 1988. "Gila Pueblo Archaeological Foundation: A History and Some Personal Notes." *Kiva,* Arizona Archaeological and Historical Society, 54(1).

Hays-Gilpin, Kelley, Emory Sekaquaptewa and Dorothy K. Washburn. 2006. "Murals and Metaphors: Introduction." *Plateau,* Museum of Northern Arizona, 3(1):17-11.

———— and Emory Sekaquaptewa. 2006. "Síitálpuva: Through the Land Brightened with Flowers." *Plateau*, Museum of Northern Arizona, 3(1):12-25.

Hodge, Carle. 1982. "Museum of Northern Arizona: The Showplace Where History Lives." *Arizona Highways*, 58(6).

National Parks and Conservation Association. 1986. "The Latest Word: Interior Honors Danson, Hart for Conservation." *National Parks*, 60(9-10):6.

Northern Arizona University. 2006. "Sharing anthropology professor benefits NAU and museum." *Inside NAU*, 3(38).

Peplow, Ed. 1957. "Northern Arizona Society of Science and Art." *Arizona Highways*, 33(6):32-38.

Roberts, David. 1992. "At Casa Malpais, Catacombs and Collaboration," *Smithsonian Magazine*, 22(12):28-34.

Thompson, Raymond H. 2001. "Obituaries: Edward Bridge Danson (1916-2000)," *American Anthropologist*, 103(4):1136-1144.

————. 2004. "How Pancho Villa and Emil Haury Established Highway Salvage Archaeology." *Journal of the Southwest*, 46(1):121-127.

Unknown. 1970. "Dams and Dilemmas: An exhibition to raise a lot of questions that have not been answered." *Arizona Republic* (September 27, 1970), 20,22,24-25.

————. 2006. "Dr. Kelley Hays-Gilpin Appointed Danson Chair of Anthropology." *MNA Notes*, Museum of Northern Arizona, (Fall/Winter):3.

Unpublished Material

Colorado Plateau Environmental Advisory Council (CPEAC). 1974. Draft Minutes of the May 29, 1974 Meeting of CPEAC at the Museum of Northern Arizona.

Colton, Harold S. and Emil W. Haury. 1955. Correspondence concerning possibility of hiring Edward Danson as Assistant Director of the Museum of Northern Arizona.

Danson, Edward B. 1948. "An Archaeological Survey of the Santa Cruz River Valley from the Headwaters to the Town of Tubac in Arizona."

————. 1993. *Memoirs of Edward Bridge Danson: Volume I: March 22, 1916-1960.*

Museum of Northern Arizona. 1956. Minutes of the Northern Arizona Society of Science and Art Board of Trustees Special Meeting on 31 January 1956.

————. 1974. Friends of the Museum: Minutes of Meeting on May 7, 1974.

U. S. Department of Interior. 1986. Program for 51st Honor Awards Convocation, September 26, 1986.

Walther, Eric. 1970. "Summary of Activities of Department of Environmental Studies since 3 August 1970: A Quarterly Report." Museum of Northern Arizona.

Museum of Northern Arizona Reports and Columns

Colton, Harold S. 1950-1958. 21st-31st Annual Report of the Director. *Plateau*, Museum of Northern Arizona.

Danson, Edward B. 1959-1974. 32nd-46th Annual Report of the Director. *Plateau*, Museum of Northern Arizona.

—————. 1973-1975. "Notes from the Director." *Museum Notes*, Museum of Northern Arizona, New Series.

EDWARD BRIDGE DANSON CORRESPONDENCE

Colton, Harold S.
Danson, Ann Allen
Danson, Jessica MacMaster
Gladwin, Dr. and Mrs. Harold
Gove, Doreen
Harvey, Daggett
Haury, Emil W.
Hayden, Senator Carl
Goldwater, Senator Barry
Perin, Virginia Danson
Muhlhauser, Robert F. and Ann Danson
Percival, Don
Smith, Watson
Smurthwaite, Carolann
Stewart, Omar C.
Wasley, William W.
Withers, Arnold

DANSON FAMILY MEMORABILIA

1916-2000	Family scrapbooks
1933-1935	Edward B. Danson's journals from University of Arizona Summer Field School at Forestdale, Arizona
1942-1944	Edward B. Danson's World War II journals and letters to Ann Allen Danson, Virginia

	Perin, Ann Danson Muhlhauser and Jessica MacMaster Danson
1933-1964	Edward B. Danson's miscellaneous letters to Ann Allen Danson, Virginia Perin, Ann Danson Muhlhauser and Jessica Mac-Master Danson
1947-1949	Edward B. Danson's journals from summer archaeological surveys of west-central New Mexico and east-central Arizona
1993	Edward B. Danson's notes for a talk: "The Hopi Indians of Arizona"
1994-?	Edward B. Danson handwritten notes for "Memoirs of Edward Bridge Danson: Volume II: 1960+"
1942-2000	Jessica MacMaster Danson correspondence with family members
2000-2001	Condolence letters to Jessica Danson following the death of Edward B. Danson

WRITTEN TRIBUTES TO NED DANSON
FOR THE CELEBRATION OF HIS LIFE
HELD ON OCTOBER 20, 2001
AT THE MUSEUM OF NORTHERN ARIZONA, FLAGSTAFF

Carothers, Steven W.
Cook, John E.
Lindsay, Alexander J.
Lipe, William and June
Lungé, Eileen and Pam Lungé
Miller, Diane
Perin, Cynthia
Perin, Dan and Laura
Thompson, Raymond H.

ACKNOWLEDGEMENTS

Telling the story of one remarkable man required the efforts of many people over the course of a year. More than anyone else, I must thank Jan Danson Haury, my mother and the daughter of this biography's subject. The idea for the book was hers, and she served as chief researcher, first editor, co-writer of the foreword and sole writer of the afterword. I must also thank my father, Loren Haury, for help with editing as well as work on the photographs and layout.

I am also grateful to all those who helped edit the book: Dr. Raymond Thompson and his wife Molly provided a thorough review of the facts and the narrative, while Bennie Blake did a masterful job of editing. Dr. Robert Breunig, Karen Enyedy and Dr. David Wilcox of the Museum of Northern Arizona brought to the book their knowledge of writing and of the Museum as an institution. And each of the other readers—Diane Miller, Joan Wentz and Bill and Patti Welter—brought their own valuable insights.

I also thank Dr. Jefferson Reid for providing information about the Mogollon controversy and for giving permission to adapt and use his map of archaeological sites in Arizona and adjacent states.

Jonathan Pringle, archivist at the Harold S. Colton Library at the Museum of Northern Arizona, gave generously of his time in locating Ned Danson's correspondence and other written materials, and sorting through photographs from the Museum's collection to illustrate this book.

Additional photographs were generously provided by Agnese Haury, Cindy Perin and Ed Chamberlin of Hubbell Trading

Post. And I am especially grateful to Pam Lungé for granting use of one of her father's paintings.

Cindy Perin shared with me her story of the challenging road trip with her "Uncle Ned," and her brother E. B. D. "Dan" Perin clarified his own role in the story of his uncle's life.

Painter and photographer John Farnsworth, a former Museum of Northern Arizona assistant curator, gave permission to use a quotation from his website.

Lulu Santamaria helped with production and gave advice on the world of publishing. Additional invaluable guidance about both writing and publishing came from Joe and Kris Neri of Sedona's Well Red Coyote Bookstore. Sheila Tressler of the Sedona Public Library provided generous assistance with cataloguing information and formatting.

Dr. Robert Breunig, Director of the Museum of Northern Arizona, has my gratitude for his support for this project, for his help with the manuscript, for taking a chance in allowing me to be the book's author and for writing the introduction.

And no list of acknowledgments for this book would be complete without recognizing my uncle, Ted Danson, for sharing his stories of his father's and mother's lives, co-writing the book's foreword, reading and commenting on the manuscript and providing support for this project.

ILLUSTRATION CREDITS

Most of the photographs and illustrations in this book are from family scrapbooks, including the pictures from the cruise of the schooner *Yankee* and some from Museum of Northern Arizona events. Photographs of archaeological field schools at Forestdale, Arizona and Point of Pines, Arizona are from family scrapbooks and are also in the Arizona State Museum archives.

THE FOLLOWING PHOTOGRAPHS ARE FROM THE MUSEUM OF NORTHERN ARIZONA'S COLLECTION:

Page 69 (top). Watson Smith, 1948. Courtesy of Museum of Northern Arizona, N-7.1948.1

Page 82 (top). Dr. Colton breaking ground for the new Research Center, 15 May 1953. Courtesy of Museum of Northern Arizona, N-8C.1953.1

Page 88. Edward Bridge Danson, 1956. Courtesy of Museum of Northern Arizona, N-7.1956.2

Page 93 (top). Hopi Craftsman Show, 1959. Ned Danson, Mary-Russell Ferrell Colton judging. Courtesy of Museum of Northern Arizona, C-100A.1959.18, Parker Hamilton

Page 113. Dr. Colton and Dr. Danson, 1958. Courtesy of Museum of Northern Arizona, N-8C.1958.1, William Belknap

Page 114. Dr. Edward B. Danson in his office, 1969. Courtesy of Museum of Northern Arizona, N-7.1969.18, G. Abbeloos

Page 132 (bottom). Edwin H. Colbert, Geology, 1975. Courtesy of Museum of Northern Arizona, N-7.1973.3

Page 137. E. B. Danson individual correspondence file. Courtesy of Museum of Northern Arizona, Withers_1955-01, Arnold Withers

Back cover. Jimmie Kewanwytewa and E.B. Danson at Jimmy K's birthday and retirement, 1961. Courtesy of Museum of Northern Arizona, N-2.1961.21, Paul Long

OTHER PHOTOGRAPHS AND ILLUSTRATIONS:

Front cover. Ned Danson at Lehner Ranch mammoth kill site, 1977. Courtesy of photographer Helga Teiwes

Page 109 (top). Hubbell Trading Post rug room. Courtesy of photographer George H. H. Huey

Pages 109 (bottom). Ned Danson and Mrs. Hubbell examining a rug at Hubbell Trading Post. Courtesy of Ed Chamberlin, Hubbell Trading Post National Historic Site

Page 122. Painting, *Home from the Sing*, by Jeffrey Lungé. Courtesy of Ted Danson, Mary Steenburgen and Pam Lungé

Page 146. Wedding photograph of Loren and Jan Haury and their parents at wedding reception, 1967. Courtesy of photographer Helga Teiwes

Page 168. Wedding photograph of Mary Steenburgen and Ted Danson with their children, 1995. Courtesy of Ted Danson and Mary Steenburgen

Page opposite table of contents. Map of Arizona. Adapted with permission from J. Jefferson Reid and Stephanie Whittlesey, *The Archaeology of Ancient Arizona*. Tucson: The University of Arizona Press, 1997

ERIC PENNER HAURY

Eric Penner Haury is a freelance writer
and grandson of Ned and Jessica Danson.
As a child, he stayed several weeks each
year with the Dansons, who regularly took
him to the Museum of Northern Arizona.
He can be contacted at:
ep_haury@yahoo.com.

CPSIA information can be obtained
at www.ICGtesting.com
Printed in the USA
FSHW011951251119
64511FS